The Pregnant Man

The Pregnant Man

And Other Cases from a Hypnotherapist's Couch

Deirdre Barrett, Ph.D.

Faculty, Harvard Medical School

TIMES BOOKS

RANDOM HOUSE

Library of Congress Cataloging-in-Publication Data

Barrett, Deirdre.
    The pregnant man: and other cases from a hypnotherapist's couch / Deirdre Barrett.
        p.   cm.
    Includes index.
    ISBN 0-8129-2905-5 (hardcover: alk. paper)
    1. Hypnotism—Therapeutic use—Case studies. I. Title.
RC497.B38   1998
616.89'162—dc21   97-46345

Design Meryl Sussman Levavi/Digitext

Random House website address: www.randomhouse.com

Printed in the United States of America

9 8 7 6 5 4 3 2

First Edition

Contents

Introduction

Franz Mesmer conducted his healing sessions in a dimly lit, plush-carpeted parlor decorated with arcane astrological symbols and hung with mirrors to reflect unseen energies. For individual treatments, he sat directly in front of his patient, fixed him—or usually her—with a penetrating gaze, and intoned repeatedly, "Go deep into your mind." When treating groups, Mesmer moved among his subjects in a purple silk robe, waving a magnetic wand and murmuring until, one by one, they swooned into trance. He passed his hands over ailing body parts, telling the blind that they would see, the deaf that they would hear, the paralyzed that they would move again. Often they did.

Psychologists would name this phenomenon first "mesmerism" for its discoverer and later "hypnotism" after the Greek god of sleep. Mesmer himself called it "animal magnetism" and attributed his success to the energy field of his hands. His flamboyant style and high rate of cures attracted notoriety across late eighteenth-century Europe. In Vienna, Mozart befriended him, performed in Mesmer's garden, and lauded him by name in the opera *Così fan tutte*. When Mesmer moved to Paris, Marie Antoinette invited him to court for repeated demonstrations of animal magnetism.

Young doctors flocked to him, eager to become apprentice magnetizers. However, established physicians of that time were no more welcoming to nontraditional healers with cult followings than they are today. Conventional neurologists had little success treating the hysterical neuroses that constituted the majority of Mesmer's cures, so they were skeptical. The French Royal Academy of Science and Medicine appointed a commission to investigate whether Mesmer should be allowed to continue his practice. The commission was chaired by American Ambassador Benjamin Franklin, and included physician Joseph Guillotin (who five years later would invent the execution device), chemist Antoine Lavoisier, and astronomer Jean Bailly (both of whom would die nine years later at the guillotine).

The investigation focused on the theory of animal magnetism and barely took note of the high rate of cures, which the commission acknowledged. Though Mesmer healed hysterics (and even cancer in a few of the cases the commission documented), the official report concluded: "No evidence could be found for the existence of a magnetic fluid and therefore no therapy could be based on it. All the reported effects are simply due to the overexcited imaginations of the subjects." No one—neither Mesmer nor any of his critics—thought it remarkable that imagination could cure so dramatically. Nor did they realize the import of discovering a technique that could "overexcite" it to cure predictably.

Mesmer left Paris in disgrace to live out the remainder of his life in the obscurity of the Swiss countryside—thereby escaping the guillotine that claimed the majority of the Parisian aristocracy. His young disciples were temporarily intimidated out of practicing magnetism, but with the onset of the French Revolution they fled to England, the United States, Germany, and Austria, where magnetism evolved into hypnotism and the role of verbal suggestion replaced the primacy of magnetic wands.

Of course, Mesmer did not invent trance, he merely rediscovered techniques that have been practiced around the world since the dawn of history. The ancient Egyptian Demotic Papyrus describes how a boy was induced into a healing trance by eye fixation on a lighted lamp. Greek temples dedicated to Asclepius—the god whose snake-entwined staff is now our modern medical symbol, the caduceus—used hypnotic incubation rituals to produce their dramatic cures. Tribal shamans from Africa to Siberia enter themselves into trance and induce it in others for healing. Mesmer's great contribution was that he reminded the Western world of this marvelous therapy, and we have remained fascinated by it since.

Hypnosis is a powerful manifestation of many unconscious powers of the mind and a dramatic metaphor for all our untapped potential. Strangely, hypnotists today often prefer to dispel this aura that Mesmer and the shamans used so effectively, assuming it may be frightening or off-putting. "Hypnosis is nothing mysterious," begins the typical modern hypnosis article or lecture. "It is completely scientific." Perhaps this is just a twist on the same routine, as science has become the focus of faith in our time. But in my practice, I like to maintain a hint of mystery. After all, people come to hypnotherapy to connect with some unknown potential within themselves—even though it may be as mundane as the potential to put aside their cigarettes. And there are those cases where, after one hypnotherapy session, a long-term smoker will throw away her pack as effortlessly as Mesmer's paralyzed hysterics walked again. Admittedly, for others, repeated sessions are only one tool in the process.

The most common misconception in hypnosis lore is the notion that trance, hallucinatory imagery, the will to carry out suggestions—indeed, all the phenomena of hypnosis—emanate from the hypnotist. In fact, it is the subject who produces these. The people who are most hypnotizable are those who engage in informal trancelike activities in their everyday lives, even if they do not realize or control them. People who had imaginary companions as children, who still automatically shut out external stimuli readily, who become absorbed in vivid fantasies are likely to be highly hypnotizable. So are those susceptible to external imagery—people who shiver when they look at a travel poster of snowy ski slopes or become queasy watching a film set on a tossing submarine. Highly hypnotizable people may even develop symptoms such as false pregnancy (as we'll see in Chapter 4), and hypnosis can be harnessed to reverse these. Fortunately, to benefit from hypnosis, it isn't necessary to be in a deep trance—except in the rare instances when hypnosis is used as the only anesthesia during major surgery. For most hypnotherapy, a light trance requiring only the bit of imagination most people possess is quite sufficient.

Although I have emphasized the "hypnosis" half of the term, the other half—"therapy"—is also a powerful ritual for change today. Because hypnosis bypasses the conscious mind's habits and resistances, it is often quicker than other forms of therapy. Therefore, its benefits may appear more dramatically. However, even in standard psychotherapy, a relatively few hours of delicate interpersonal dance can effect changes of lasting import. The reputed dangers of hypnotherapy are really those of all therapy: first, that an overzealous therapist may push the patient to face what has been walled off for good reason before new strengths are in place, and second, that the therapist will abuse her—or more often his—position of persuasion. People come to hypnotherapy with many of the identical complaints and hopes that they bring to any treatment for physical or psychological problems. Despite the added role of hypnotizability, most of the same factors determine the outcome: the skill of the therapist, the patient's motivation to drop old patterns, the rapport between patient and therapist, and how supportive family and friends are of change.

I'm often asked how I became interested in hypnosis. I remember being fascinated by it from childhood—as were so many other children. Slumber parties became the rage when I was in sixth grade. Along with ghost stories, Ouija boards, and discussions of boys, our attempts to hypnotize one another ranked high as entertainment after we had been told to turn off the lights. Despite our clumsy technique, giggling, and faking of responses, a couple of highly hypnotizable girls actually went into deep trances—to our delight then, and to my alarm in retrospect. Rather than "becoming" interested in this dramatic phenomenon, I just never lost interest en route to choosing a grown-up career. In my undergraduate psychology courses, I delved further into the subject and, more exciting, I got to be a subject for hypnosis research at a local hospital. Long-forgotten details of minor events in my early life came back vividly when the hypnotist suggested age regression. As he awakened me, I remember a sense of emerging from great depths. Dreams were the closest analogy I could find, but hypnosis felt like a dream with considerably more direction. This experience of hallucinatory perceptions coexisting with logical, waking reason intensified my interest.

I selected a clinical psychology program and then an internship that had hypnosis courses (fewer than one in ten of either did). I studied hypnotic inductions, rehearsing them out loud in characteristic slow, soothing tones. Classmates and I practiced these first on one another, then on undergraduate volunteers. Each time a new suggestion worked—from the simplest, making our eyelids so heavy, to difficult ones, such as seeing a person who was not actually there (positive hallucination) or blotting out a person who really was (negative hallucination)—I wondered if the subjects were putting me on. Quickly, I realized that their amazement at how *I* did that was as great as mine at how *they* did. Trance ability resides in the subject, but it is the skill of the hypnotist that draws it out.

After I had practiced a variety of suggestions on volunteers for a while, my first outpatient practicum allowed me to begin using hypnotherapy. I found that many complaints—smoking, overeating, test anxiety, public speaking phobia, and chronic physical pain—responded more dramatically to hypnosis than to the other forms of psychotherapy I was using. Sometimes it worked by uncovering deep underlying causes, other times by direct, almost simpleminded suggestions. I did my dissertation research on hypnotic imagery, comparing it with night dreams (which, not surprisingly, have more "dreamlike" distortions, more unpleasant emotions, more family members as characters, and many references to the distant past) and with daydreams (which feature more logical story lines, pleasant emotions, more friends, and are usually set in the present or immediate future). I found that most people's hypnotic imagery fell between their nocturnal dreams and daydreams on these dimensions. For a few of the deepest trance subjects, hypnotic imagery was every bit as "dreamlike" as their night dreams and was even accompanied by rapid eye movements indistinguishable from those that lend the name REM to the stage of sleep in which dreams occur.

Since receiving my Ph.D. in 1979, I have conducted research identifying personality traits that predict the type of hypnotic induction to which a patient is likely to respond best. I've also studied the childhood experiences that characterize two main types of highly hypnotizable people (more on this last topic in the conclusion). I teach hypnotherapy in my job at Harvard Medical School and at national and international workshops, and I supervise hypnotherapy and hypnosis research. I've always maintained an active clinical practice—in both hypnotherapy and more general forms of psychotherapy—because I believe teachers and researchers should not become removed from actual experience and because hypnotherapy continues to be a fascinating and rewarding endeavor.

This is a casebook of seven patients I have treated over those two decades. The stories are in chronological order from my trainee days to the present, so that the reader may follow the journey by which I learned about hypnosis. I have deviated from fact only as necessary for patient confidentiality. Most changes are of incidental details—names, physical descriptions, occupations, locales, dates of treatment. On the few occasions when something more central to the case might be identifiable to the reader, I have substituted an element from the life of a similar patient so that the story remains true to the therapeutic process. In certain cases, the patient depicted is a composite of patients with similar issues. This enabled me to report therapy conversation directly along with gestures, expressions, and other minutiae of a psychologically significant but less traceable nature.

I have resisted the temptation to present only the stories of patients who were cured, as there are always some treatment failures in any practice. The common pitfall of describing only positive progress occurs in hospital treatment summaries as well as published case studies. It is probably attributable more to therapists' tendencies to delude themselves than to any intent of deceiving the audience. Freud is the most notorious example of this, largely because he became so famous that historians and biographers uncovered the identities of his poorly disguised patients. When Freud changed details, it was often to protect Victorian sensibilities rather than individual confidentiality: incestuous relations with fathers were converted into ones with uncles, governesses, and friends of the family in multiple cases. Among his more famous cases who were later identified—Dora, Irma, "the Wolf Man," and Little Hans—long-term outcomes ranged from those still hospitalized (with more severe forms of the disorders that Freud had allegedly successfully analyzed) to functioning professionals with lingering doubts about whether Freud had anything to do with the changes that occurred during the years of their contact with him.

The most bizarre of the cases set forth by analyst Robert Lindner in his 1954 classic, *The Fifty-Minute Hour,* is a physicist with delusions that he is from a distant solar system. He is portrayed in the book as having been cured by analysis. In fact, for the remainder of his life, he experienced the same manic-depressive episodes. (This condition is now known to be largely biological; lithium would probably have landed him quickly on earth.) I happen to know the postscript of this case only because I grew up in the government research town that housed the nuclear laboratory where this severely disturbed man had helped to develop the atomic bomb. His reputed analytic "cure" was a source of some amusement there because remarkably decorative maps of his planet of origin—drawn long after his analysis by Lindner—still hung on the walls of private residences and in the city art gallery. A better-known example of the premature announcement of a "cure" is Christine Costner Sizemore, the multiple personality described as integrated in *The Three Faces of Eve,* a

1957 best-seller written by her first psychiatrist, Corbett Thigpen, and his supervisor, Hervey Cleckley. In 1989, Sizemore published *A Mind of My Own,* a memoir of her continuing struggles with more than a dozen personalities long after that first therapy.

In the interest of portraying a realistic range of outcomes, I have included one case involving the kind of total treatment failure that leaves me puzzling twenty years later about what I might have done differently (see Chapter 2). Even with dramatic successes, I have tried to communicate the omnipresent possibility that change is temporary or incomplete. It has been my intention in these case studies to keep sight of the inevitable limitations and uncertainties of hypnotherapy while conveying the excitement I feel about the potential of psychotherapy in general and hypnosis in particular.

How did I choose which patients' stories to include? Occasionally, therapy unfolds like a play, with me at times audience, at other times actor, but never holding more than a fragment of the script. A colorful character walks in and presents a problem, there are several unexpected twists in the plot, and a solution arrives climactically (or fails climactically, as I've just alluded to). The following seven stories are among the most dramatic instances I've experienced of imagination "overexcited" to heal.

The Pregnant Man

1
The Counterfeit
Adult

Nancy Jordan sat down in my University Health Service office and lit a cigarette. The habit was deadly, given her severe asthma and tobacco allergies. Nancy's petite build, blond pixie cut, and girlish demeanor suggested a child sneaking a smoke at recess, although she was actually a lovely young woman. Jonathan Hunter, M.D.—my supervisor, her psychotherapist—sat in the room with us. He'd said he was attending the first hypnotherapy session to put the shy college sophomore at ease. I knew he was also eager to observe hypnosis. "Hunter," as he was known to everyone from his patients to his wife, was supervising my graduate school psychotherapy practicum. However, it was I who had taken a hypnosis course and practiced on volunteers for a semester of the previous year. Our agreement was that he, as a nonhypnotist, would direct me on general psychological aspects of my first hypnotherapy case.

Along with a jacket and tie, Hunter wore jeans and cowboy boots, reflecting his Texas roots. The undergraduates enjoyed his informality. At thirty-five, he was young enough to identify with their issues but old enough to be an authority to them and, for that matter, to me. Hunter positioned his chair behind the recliner in which Nancy sat, as if he were simply going to watch, but he spoke up more often than his patient. "She was admitted to the hospital in status asthmaticus twice last month," he told me. "Her condition is getting worse fast."

"I know, I know," Nancy acknowledged meekly. Her jeans, T-shirt, and sneakers were at the casual end of campus attire. With no makeup on her blue-eyed, lightly freckled face, she appeared even younger than her nineteen years. The University of Tennessee Health Service required Hunter and me to do all evaluations. However, we were expected to refer most students needing therapy to private practitioners; health insurance was still generous in 1977. That gave us much control over who we saw. The majority of Hunter's patients were unusually attractive coeds, although I never got any hint of inappropriate self-indulgence beyond his initial visual selection. I was taking advantage of the process in my own way by picking students I thought were good teaching cases.

In his smooth drawl, Hunter had filled me in about Nancy's family before the session. Nancy was the middle of three children. She and her older sister, Meg, had been inseparable through childhood, but Meg was now living in San Diego and estranged from their family because her fundamentalist Christian parents violently objected to her Jewish boyfriend. Nancy had never gotten along well with her younger brother, Jimmy, now in high school. Her mother was a housewife and "difficult." Most important for Hunter, Nancy's adored father was a physician—a prominent neurosurgeon at a teaching hospital in Atlanta. I already knew that the medical profession was a fraternity of sorts, with a loyalty that, for better or worse, I had not seen among my fellow psychologists. The children of M.D.'s were also heavily represented among Hunter's patients.

Nancy dutifully recited the details of starting to smoke at fifteen and reaching her present two packs a day by age eighteen. She was majoring in journalism, made good grades, had a lot of friends, and was going steady with a "really cool guy." Hunter rolled his eyes at this last statement, which made me wonder what else he knew. Nancy lived in an off-campus apartment with one roommate and had just last week acquired Rags, a white poodle puppy—the one breed to which she was not allergic. Nancy painted a picture of a happy life disrupted only by the frightening episodes in which her windpipe spasmed shut.

Having gathered enough background information for the hypnosis, I positioned my desk chair at a ninety-degree angle to the recliner in which my young patient sat. Hunter remained behind her, to the side of my view, but I was very conscious of him watching us.

I asked Nancy to look up at the ceiling, where four porous white tiles intersected in a neat point. I have yet to encounter a hypnotist who employs the swinging gold pocket watch depicted in films and on television as a focal point, though much of the rest of those Hollywood inductions is accurate. Instead, we ask subjects to gaze at a steady object to block distracting visual stimuli. The point selected is often above the head in order to tire the eyes faster. Gazing up has another trance-inducing property: it causes more alpha in the brain waves. Alpha is the frequency associated with deep relaxation. The only other simple way to increase alpha quickly is by closing the eyes—which, of course, I would ask the patient to do further into the hypnotic induction.

"Stare at the point on the ceiling, and let your breathing become slow and deep. Let your body begin to relax, starting with the muscles of your feet and toes . . . let them relax. Let your ankles relax . . . let your calves relax . . . let all the muscles around your knees relax." I timed the rhythm of my speech to the rise and fall of her breathing. "Let your thighs relax; let all tension flow out of your legs until they're as limp and loose as those of a rag doll." This is a useful metaphor to induce patients to let go of muscle tone if they still have positive associations with dolls. Nancy had impressed me as childlike in her bubbling delight over her new puppy. Little did I know just how accurate this first impression would prove.

"Let your hips relax. Allow the relaxation to spread up through your back, letting go of all the tension there. Let the muscles across your stomach relax. . . . Let your chest relax so that it becomes easier to breathe slowly and deeply with almost no effort at all." I kept my voice soothing and slow, hoping it did not betray any of the self-consciousness I felt, aware of Hunter's form in the periphery of my vision.

"Let the relaxation spread down into your shoulders. . . ." I had been timing my words with her breathing but as I talked her through the remaining muscle groups, I gradually slowed my voice so that her breathing would have a subliminal cue to slow down also. When I got to her face, I suggested more passive activity: "Feel the muscles of your cheeks relax, the muscles of your jaw, and all the muscles around your mouth relaxing completely, until your whole face feels very limp . . . and loose . . . and comfortable.

"As you continue to stare at the point on the ceiling, your eyelids are becoming heavier, as if a weight were attached, pulling them gently down. You may notice the point start to move around or change color or somehow look different; that will be a sign you are beginning to go into hypnosis as your eyelids get heavier and heavier. Each time you blink, it gets harder to open your eyes again at all. Soon they will close completely, and you will sink into a peaceful, sleeplike state." Nancy looked drowsy, and her eyes began to droop.

At that point I glanced over at Hunter to see what he thought of the induction. The worst my insecure imagination conjured up was mild disapproval, but what greeted my eyes was infinitely more dismaying. My big, rangey supervisor sat slumped in his chair. His eyes were closed, muscles completely lax, his breathing barely detectable.

My induction stalled as I wondered what to do next. Nancy rested silently, not seeming to notice the delay. I resumed my monologue to her, internally debating my course of action. "Your eyelids are getting heavier. . . ." Briefly I considered that, once her eyes closed, I could just proceed, ignoring Hunter. I had no idea, however, how a nonsmoker in a trance would receive instructions about "your smoking." At the extreme, I feared Hunter would awaken thinking he did smoke. He also leaned at such an angle that he was at risk of slipping out of the narrow chair. I imagined winding up with a supervisor with a concussion or at least a patient awakened with a *thud* of disconcerting origins. As I continued to talk about heaviness, Nancy's eyelids opened sluggishly only halfway when she blinked. I decided that a generally phrased wake-up suggestion at this point would innocuously end both their trances without seeming odd to Nancy.

"Good, you've experienced how to get very relaxed and ready to enter hypnosis. In a minute, I am going to count from ten to one backwards. As I do, the heaviness will leave your body and you will feel yourself gradually returning to the waking state. By the count of 'one,' you will be alert and refreshed as if you'd had a long nap. You may carry a bit of the relaxation with you if you wish, but you will be focused and ready for the rest of the day. Ten . . . nine . . . ."

Nancy's eyelids gradually opened wider and the sleepy expression left her face. At the count of "one," Hunter's eyes popped opened. He pulled himself upright in the chair, appearing momentarily confused. He quickly affected a look of exaggerated nonchalance.

"What was that like?" I asked Nancy.

"I felt very relaxed. It was as if my body was melting into the chair. My eyes did feel like weights were attached. I think I was about to close them. It was very pleasant, but then I would get a little self-conscious and kind of fight it."

"Well, this was enough to tell us that hypnosis will

work well with you. As you get used to it, you probably won't feel like fighting it. Are you ready to schedule an appointment for just the two of us to begin working on the smoking?"

"Yes."

"Is that all right with you, Hunter?"

"Uh, oh, sure," he replied in a painstakingly casual voice.

Nancy and I agreed to meet the following Wednesday. "I'm so glad you are doing this," she told me effusively as she backed out the door. "I don't know what I'd do about the smoking otherwise."

"You were out cold!" I announced to Hunter the instant the door closed behind Nancy.

He dropped the look of nonchalance, and the perplexity reappeared. "I think I dozed off."

"You woke up with the count of 'one,' which was no louder than the rest of my speech. You must have been hypnotized. Don't you remember anything?" People do fall into normal sleep sometimes from the relaxation of a hypnotic induction, but if that happens they don't awaken until the hypnotist raises his or her voice or even shakes them lightly—things I was grateful I had not had to do in front of Nancy.

"I hadn't meant to, but I was looking at the ceiling when you mentioned it might look different. The X between the tiles was changing color, and the tiles would suddenly look dark for a moment and the X would be light." This sounded like a highly hypnotizable person's reaction. "I remember you saying my eyes would close by

themselves, er, I mean, her eyes would close," Hunter corrected himself. "I don't remember shutting them, but I
must have. Next thing I remember, you said 'one,' and I
knew I'd missed something. Maybe I *was* hypnotized."
This was as close as Hunter ever came to acknowledging
the difficult position in which he'd placed me.

"How do you feel now?"

"Great, like I've had a long, refreshing nap," he said,
echoing my words, apparently unconsciously.

Very hypnotizable people have the ability to go into a
trance in response to rudimentary inductions, including
ones not aimed at them. The hypnotist's skill accounts for
only a small percentage of the results. The subject's natural trance ability determines a much larger portion.

In a study I was later to do on highly hypnotizable
people, one of my subjects, when asked whether she had
ever been hypnotized before, replied, "Maybe." She described an incident in which she and her boyfriend had
watched a police show on television. There was a scene
of hypnosis with a witness. The detective began to tell the
witness to fall into a deep sleep. My subject didn't remember anything after that until she awoke with a start
and demanded confusedly, "What happened?" some
twenty minutes later. Her boyfriend told her that the show
had continued with questions during the hypnosis, several
scenes of what other characters were doing elsewhere, a
commercial break, and then returned to the detective
bringing the witness out of the trance. My subject had apparently roused out of deep hypnosis with that command.
I am now accustomed to such phenomena, but I was totally unprepared at the time for Hunter's impromptu
trance.

The following week, Nancy suffused the office with acrid smoke from her cigarette even before she spoke. "I had a bad episode of asthma just last night, although I didn't have to go to the hospital. The inhaler finally got it under control."

"Well, we'll tackle the smoking with today's hypnosis as soon as you're ready."

"I'm ready," she said. I gestured at the cigarette in her hand. "Oh, yeah." She laughed and blushed. She took one more quick drag and stubbed it out.

I again had her sit back in the recliner. "Look up at the point where the tiles intersect. Begin to let your body relax. . . ." I talked her through the same relaxation sequence. As her eyes started to droop, I said, "Eventually your lids will become so heavy that you can't keep them open any longer." Her eyes closed on cue.

"Your body can relax completely as your mind begins to float into a sleeplike state, far from your usual thoughts and concerns. You may find that you still occasionally hear some other sound around you or an everyday thought may pass through your mind for a moment, but these things do not need to distract you. You will find it easy to let go of them and bring your attention back to my voice and to the things I am suggesting for you to experience.

"The first thing I want you to picture in your mind's eye is a staircase, as if you were standing at the top looking down at a landing below. Notice whether the staircase is curved or straight, whether it is modern or ancient, familiar or exotic. You can observe what the stairs are made of—whether they are wooden, or stone, covered with carpet or some other material." I always give specifics for concrete images in this "deepening" stage, since some subjects have difficulty generating this kind of detail for themselves. For good imagers, it may at first lead to seeing each alternative briefly, but one picture will gradually crystallize.

"You can look at the handrail and see whether it is wooden or metal or made of something else, whether it is ornately carved or simple, whether it feels warm or cool. You can notice if there is a wall next to the stairs, whether it is painted, covered with wallpaper, or paneled. Look at where the light is coming from, whether it is bright or dim, natural or artificial. Note if there are any special sounds or smells that go with standing at the top of the stairs." Just as in dreams, most imagery in hypnosis is visual. A few people, however, experience more sounds or movement, and deep trance subjects may have a completely multimodal experience. Therefore, it is important to include something for each sense.

"In a moment, you are going to walk down the staircase in your mind's eye. You will find that each step takes you deeper and deeper into a peaceful, sleeplike state, further and further from your usual thoughts and surroundings until, when you reach the bottom of the stairs, you will be very deeply asleep. Then I want you to signal me by raising the index finger of your left hand for a minute and letting it go back to rest on the chair. Go ahead and walk down the stairs."

"Down" is a common hypnotic metaphor for journeying into the unconscious. Meditative traditions often use imagery of "up" to denote altering one's state of consciousness. This may make a subtle difference, because "up" often symbolizes transcendence or the future, whereas "down" is associated with things baser, or past. However, the directions share the symbolism of journeying from one's usual plane of existence. Nancy's left index finger slowly lifted off the arm of the chair, as if floating without volition.

"Now I want you to turn your attention to your smoking. I am going to ask you if you really wish to quit. Instead of thinking about this consciously, I want you to relax and let your unconscious mind answer by raising your left index finger for yes, or your right index finger for no." With less psychologically minded patients, I would use "the back of your mind" or some other phrase instead of "unconscious mind" to match their vocabulary. But Nancy had already been in a year of therapy, and she was certainly familiar with Freudian terminology. "Now let your unconscious answer me: Are you ready to quit smoking?"

This time it was Nancy's right finger that slowly raised and lowered. I had been told that a no response would be rare, but here it was, in my very first hypnotherapy case. I proceeded cautiously. "You can have some thoughts about why you are not ready to quit smoking. Relax and see what comes to mind. You will find that you can speak slowly and clearly while remaining deeply asleep. Now, tell me why you are not ready."

In a plaintive voice, remarkably like that of a six-year-old child, Nancy lisped, "Because that's the only time I feel like a gwown-up." I was accustomed to varying degrees of realistic enactment of age regression from the practice in my course, but this took me by surprise—partly be-

----

cause I had not suggested it and also because Nancy sounded more childlike than anyone I had so far encountered.

"You will be able to have some thoughts and images about other things that would make you feel grown up. Again, you won't need to think about it effortfully; just watch what comes to mind." After a few moments of silence, I said, "Now just tell me what images or thoughts are there about what else makes you feel grown-up."

"I feel like a gwown-up when I wear makeup and dresses and high heels. I feel like a gwown-up when I use big words. I feel like a gwown-up when I do my hands like this"—Nancy pressed all five fingertips of each hand to the corresponding opposite ones and rotated them back and forth while her face assumed a mock-solemn expression, obviously imitating a mannerism of some admired adult.

Although Hunter's presence had made me self-conscious the week before, I now wished he was here to nod "go ahead" or "stop" or perhaps to question Nancy himself. I had to proceed with my beginner's tools. Symptom substitution is a technique therapists use to identify something that can meet the same need as a problem behavior. A superficial example for someone who wants to stop smoking is the use of chewing gum for oral gratification. Nancy's needs were more symbolic. If she was a healthier patient who smoked less, it might have been most important to help her feel more genuinely adult without props. However, the immediate effect of Nancy's smoking on her asthma was the most pressing concern. She had provided me with ideal symptom substitutions, and her therapy with Hunter could address the long-term issues implicit in them.

"You are going to find now that, instead of smoking, you will be able to do one of these other things to feel like a grown-up and have no need for cigarettes." Swallowing my feminist attitudes about what adult confidence should be based on, I proceeded: "You will be able to put on a dress and heels or makeup and feel grown-up, so that it will be easy to go out and not smoke. When you are talking, if you need to feel grown-up, you'll be able to use a big word and find that the thought of a cigarette leaves your mind. You'll be able to press your fingers together, rock your hands, and be amazed at how you don't even think of smoking anymore." I added this last part because a surprise element in suggestions can underscore their effortlessness. "This will work better than cigarettes ever did. It's a grown-up way to handle asthma," I continued, employing her key motivating concept. "In the days and weeks to come, you can feel more and more confident without cigarettes. When you would have smoked, you will use one of these other things to feel adult." I phrased the degree of surrendering her habit vaguely so as not to interfere if her improvement began gradually.

Using hypnosis to help someone stop smoking usually involves age regression to the first time he or she ever smoked—how the young person coughed and felt nauseated as his or her body sensed that smoke does not belong in the lungs. Then the hypnotist suggests that the person is going to regain this natural, reflexive response and that cigarettes will taste awful if the patient does light up. However, with Nancy I focused on her major issue, of feeling grown-up. This seemed plenty for one session; I could introduce other suggestions later if necessary.

"In a moment I am going to ask you to wake up as I count backwards from ten to one. You will gradually feel yourself returning to a normal waking state. You may bring a bit of the relaxation with you if you like, but you will be alert and ready to resume the day's activities at the count of one. My suggestions and your imagery will stay with you to guide you not to smoke in the days and weeks to come. Ten . . . nine . . ."

At "one," Nancy opened her eyes. "Oh, I feel great. Did we already finish the hypnosis?"

"Yes, how much do you remember?"

"Just that you were telling me to relax and my eyes got heavy. This time they closed, I think. Then it's kind of blank until you were asking me to wake up." Most people remember everything that happened while they were hypnotized if they are not expressly instructed to forget. Many subjects remember even with such a suggestion. Spontaneous amnesia is rare. I hadn't seen it during the practice sessions for my course, but now I'd observed it twice in a row, with Hunter's blank trance of a week earlier.

"You don't remember anything about smoking?"

"No, but you must have told me that I would not want to smoke, 'cause I don't even feel like it." She put her hands together and rocked them with a thoughtful expression. This was no longer a child's imitation; it looked quite natural. I had intended to ask Nancy more about the origin of this gesture once she awoke, but I had not expected the amnesia. I didn't question it now for fear of disrupting its unconscious function.

"Usually I'd be wanting a cigarette after"—she glanced

at her watch—"My God, it's been over thirty minutes! It feels like five." Nancy had just experienced foreshortening, the most common hypnotic time distortion. Occasionally, to some patients, the session seems longer than the actual time elapsed.

"Yes, it's almost time to stop. I want to see how much you can refrain from smoking this week. I'll see you next Wednesday, and we'll do more hypnosis."

"Thank you so much," she said, almost too sweetly. "This is such a lifesaver." When someone works this hard at trying to make me feel good about myself, I always suspect that he or she has had at least one parent who was hellish when not pampered and appeased. Whatever its origin, however, Nancy's effusive gratitude warmed my ego as a novice therapist.

The following Wednesday, Nancy walked into the session wearing a powder blue knit dress and matching two-inch pumps. As best I could detect, she had added mascara and light lipstick, still tastefully within mainstream campus attire. Her demeanor was perhaps a bit older, but just as fresh and unaffected. My fear that I had created a Tammy Faye Bakker look-alike vanished.

"I haven't had a cigarette in a week. Not even a thought of one." This latter part was truly rare. Often hypnosis provides enough impetus to quit, but usually some willpower is also necessary. Nancy was among the lucky few who are so highly hypnotizable that suggestions override even physiologic withdrawal symptoms, much the way they vanquish surgical pain for the same people.

I hypnotized Nancy again, just to reinforce her use of

substitute behaviors in lieu of smoking. I usually tape-record this maintenance session for patients to listen to on their own, but Nancy's amnesia for the sessions rendered self-hypnosis less advisable—after all, how would she know if she'd practiced it? We discussed her returning if she became tempted to smoke in the future. I said I would check with Hunter that she was doing okay. Throughout this session, she occasionally used a sophisticated word that caught my attention but never seemed overblown. I wished I'd seen more of her before I'd suggested the symptom substitution to have a better sense of what, if any, changes had occurred. There did not appear to be a problem with her new speech or dress—or with the thoughtful pursing of her hands that was now one of Nancy's integral mannerisms. She thanked me effusively and shot me an idolizing glance as she departed. My first hypnosis case seemed to be wrapping up neatly.

"Why don't you take her on as a regular therapy client, since hypnosis works so well with her?" Hunter suggested when I told him of our success.

"You mean you wouldn't see her anymore?" I asked dubiously.

"I mean we would give her the choice. Nancy seems to like you, and her regular therapy is kind of stuck. She never gets beyond trying to be a good girl and please me, even though I interpret that to her. Since she is so hypno-tizable, this might be just the thing to get her working on her other problems. It's January; you could do hypnosis with her for the rest of the school year. If she needs more therapy, she could see me again next fall."

Both Nancy and I agreed to this arrangement. In our first general therapy session, I didn't use hypnosis; instead she brought me up to date on issues in her life. Out of trance, she did not describe herself as a child but rather as inept, inadequate, never able to do anything right. Nancy admired other people as much more talented, brainy, or artistic. It seemed to me that those she described just had more self-confidence. She used words like "big," "athletic," and "wise" for her boyfriend, Kurt—the way a child often views an adult. She also talked disturbingly often about what Kurt "lets me do."

In our next session we began to use hypnosis to address this problem, which she had succinctly described in trance as not feeling "like a gwown-up." I decided to employ an "affect bridge." This technique has two possible functions. The first is to use a feeling in the present—usually a negative one—to take someone back to a more important incident when she or he felt the same way, to get at the origin of the emotion. This process provides an interpretation, one that comes from the patient's own unconscious. The second possible use of an affect bridge is to start with a positive feeling the patient lacks in the present but can locate at some point in the past. Then the affect bridge is used to bring the positive emotion into his or her current life. This may be happiness for a depressive, a feeling of safety for a phobic, or—in this case—a sense of mastery and competence for an insecure adult.

After talking Nancy through the induction, I told her that she could move back to a time when she had done something successful and was pleased with herself. "Don't try to decide what this will be logically," I suggested. "Just imagine pleasure and accomplishment with doing something well. Experience that sense of achievement, and see what time and place come to mind. Can you see a scene of something great you've done?"

"I drew the zoo," she announced proudly, reverting to her childlike voice.

"Tell me about the picture."

"There's three cages I made with black crayons. In the first one is Mr. Monkey swinging from the top bar. He's all brown except for blue eyes and a pink smile. Second is Mr. Lion who is yellow with big white teeth. And, third, the baby giraffe with orange polka dots." I could almost see the boldly crayoned creatures as she described them. "I made flowers in front of the cages, red tulips and white daisies. Over at the side is the seal pond. One seal is jumping out of the water with a blue and yellow beach ball on its nose."

"That sounds beautiful. Can you tell me about the surroundings where you drew this picture?"

"I made it in the den on the floor with big paper and the Crayola box. My little brother, Jimmy, was with me trying to draw, too. Now that it's done, I get up and go looking for Mom, to show her how pretty it is."

"And do you find her?" I asked automatically.

"Yes, she's sitting at her desk writing checks. She looks mean. Usually I wouldn't interrupt her, but I think she'll like my zoo, so I say, 'See what I drew?' "

"What does your mom do?"

"She takes it and says, 'uh huh,' but then before she really looks at it, Jimmy is there. 'I drew one, too,' he says, and sticks his in front of mine. Mom tells him, 'Oh, how wonderful. You did that? It's lovely.' It is not!" Nancy's voice carries the intensity of youthful malice. "It's not even a picture! He just took one crayon and scribbled back and forth all over the paper. Mom keeps saying how great it is. She hands mine back without having looked at it. I try to give it to her again. 'Don't bother me. I told you to play in the den. I'm busy with Jimmy. You're asking for a whipping if you don't get out of here this minute, young lady!'" Nancy is sobbing now. "His is awful. She always likes anything he does. Nothing of mine is ever any good!"

This was interesting material that helped explain Nancy's insecurities, but it was certainly not strengthening her confidence in the present. I said, "Let's go back to before you went looking for your mother, to when you had just finished the picture. Go back to looking at the zoo with Mr. Monkey and Mr. Lion and the baby giraffe and the seals. Notice all the pretty flowers. Can you see your picture again?"

"Yes."

"See how well you drew everything?"

"Yes." She'd returned to her happy voice.

"Now *you* know how good it is and *I* know it, even if no one else told you. Just concentrate on finishing your picture and being proud of it, knowing what a beautiful zoo you've made. Focus on that feeling of accomplishment as you leave the picture and the den behind. Later you will be able to remember as much as you want to about it." I specified this because of her propensity for amnesia. "Stay with that happiness and pride. Let it form a bridge to carry you back to the present feeling good. In a moment, I will count backwards from ten to one. By the count of one you will be wide awake . . ."

"His drawing really was just scribble marks!" Nancy

awoke sounding sure of herself. "Mine was pretty. I really did some good art back then for a kid."

In supervision, Hunter suggested that other irrational trends, such as Nancy's propensity for guilt about things that were not her fault and her lack of assertiveness, might both respond to this approach. We used hypnosis to work on these over the next several sessions, and she seemed to be gaining confidence. Until a crisis arose.

Nancy entered our first session of March looking distraught. "I think I'm going crazy." "What's the matter?" My voice must have conveyed that I did not take this literally.

"No, *really.*" A hint of tears showed in the corners of her eyes. "I'm seeing things and hearing things."

"Like what?"

"When I try to turn the light on, it doesn't go on. I flip the light switch on and off, and nothing changes. When I turn the stereo on, there's just silence. My boyfriend, Kurt, and my roommate say they see the light go on and hear the music. Am I totally schizophrenic?"

These symptoms did sound very unusual, and Nancy was confused in a way I'd never seen her before. However, a negative hallucination, as psychologists call blocking out conscious recognition of something that is clearly perceptible, is not a sign of schizophrenia, manic psychosis, or any known organic brain syndrome. It *is,* though, common in response to hypnotic suggestion. In class demonstrations the previous year, I'd seen subjects convincingly ignore a person they'd been instructed not to perceive. One enterprising subject speculated that his arm was floating up by posthypnotic suggestion when in fact the "absent" person was lifting it.

The only mental disorder associated with these symptoms is what used to be known as hysteria and is now termed dissociative disorder. This syndrome is known to have a strong link to childhood trauma and is present in one group of highly hypnotizable people. As far back as Freud's classic hysteria cases, trancelike complaints such as paralysis and tunnel vision have been reported. These people are not "crazy" in the sense of being psychotic. They usually demonstrate good social skills, logical reasoning, and generally normal behaviors except for manifesting one or more bizarre symptoms.

"You don't have to be schizophrenic to hallucinate," I told Nancy. "As I've been telling you, highly hypnotizable people can do amazing things, and it doesn't always have to be the result of formal hypnosis. You may be doing something that's like self-hypnosis that causes you not to see these things. Some people even like to hallucinate; look at all the street drugs for that purpose." After all, this was 1975 on a college campus.

"Yes, I know; Kurt does LSD on the weekends. Some of my other friends have tried it. I've always been scared to do anything like acid or PCP or even grass. I can't imagine wanting to see things, but now I am anyway!" People with the dissociative disordered type of trance ability usually dislike mind-altering drugs. They are vigilant and want to be in control at all times. They sense that bad things lurking in their minds would take over if they were to let go of control. Flashback phenomena are common when they do drugs. However, the content of Nancy's hallucinations was not obviously unpleasant, so it was difficult to guess their origin.

"Did something special happen before you began 'seeing things'?"

"Well, there's been a huge mess this week. Dad's in the hospital."

"Oh, I'm sorry to hear that. What's wrong with him?"

"Nothing." She seemed to realize how impossible this sounded. "I mean, it's not a regular hospital. . . ." She hesitated. "He's in a psychiatric institution."

"Does that have anything to do with your being afraid you might be going crazy?"

"Of course not, *he's* not crazy. They just put him there so he wouldn't get arrested or something."

"You said there was nothing wrong?"

"Well, he drank too much. He does that sometimes."

"What did he do when he drank?"

"He'd been out all night at a bar when he showed up for six A.M. surgery. He was completely intoxicated and when he started undressing to get into his scrub suit, he was"—she hesitated longer now—"he was wearing diapers and plastic pants." Nancy's pained expression restrained my impulse to laugh.

"His partners were at the hospital. They took over the surgery and got him out of there fast so there would be no chance of anyone pressing charges or him losing his license. They had him admitted to this place out of state so it would stay anonymous."

"And that's when your problems with the light switch and stereo began?"

"Not right away. In fact, not when I was the most freaked out about it. Mom called me, all furious. She made it sound like he'd done this just to embarrass her. Also, she implied it's my fault somehow. I was really upset. But then I was able to talk to Dad at the hospital. He'd sobered up by then and sounded like himself. He can always calm me down and put things in perspective. It's not such a big deal—he just got drunk. He only has to stay in the hospital two weeks. It was later that afternoon when I wanted to listen to music that the thing with the switches first happened. It's been like that for three days now."

Nancy agreed that she'd like to work on the hallucinations with hypnosis. I put her in a trance and suggested, "You can focus on being in your room trying to turn the light switch on and off and not seeing the light. Then you are at the stereo wanting to listen to music. You turn it on and hear nothing. Your unconscious knows what this means. Can you tell me what it's about?"

"Just not to think about Dad. I'd rather think about anything else," she said in a voice that sounded a bit younger than it had just minutes ago.

"And the hallucinations distract you?"

"Yes."

"You can see some scenes or images," I suggested. "They will explain why you are afraid to think about your father's problems."

After a moment, she spoke in a completely childlike voice. "I'm in my bed asleep. All of a sudden Daddy's there, turning on the lights. My sister, Meg, who sleeps in the other bed, is already awake and sitting up. Daddy's hugging her; he comes over to me and gives me a big hug, too. He sits down on the foot of my bed. He's got two packages, all wrapped up in yellow striped paper with big white bows. He hands one to my sister and gives the other to me. We both start tearing the paper open and they are baby dolls, just alike except mine has blond hair and a blue dress and Meg's has dark hair and a purple dress. They both have baby bottles, white diapers, and little gold crowns on their heads. They're both beautiful. 'Princesses for my little princesses,' Daddy says. We're all three talking happily for a few minutes, and then Daddy says, 'Time to go back to sleep. I'll see you in the morning.' He wants to put the dolls over on the dresser, but we both want to sleep with them, so he lets us. He turns out the light and closes our door behind him. I'm not sleepy, so I keep playing with my baby doll in the dark, putting the bottle up to her mouth to feed her. Eventually I lay her down next to my cheek, and I guess I went to sleep. That's all."

Responses to memory suggestions are not easily predictable. I had expected associations with Nancy's father's problems to lead to a negative memory, yet here was an apparently happy one. Previously, the suggestion to revisit an accomplishment had led to remembering her mother's criticism. Although I recognized the elements of light switches and diapers in both this scene and Nancy's past week's experiences, it was hard to tell what to make of this recollection. I used it ambiguously in my next suggestion.

"Let the scene fade from your mind's eye, although when you wake up, you'll be able to remember as much as you want about it. You may be ready to let go of not seeing or hearing changes when you move switches. Possibly you'll be ready to think more about your dad. Or maybe you'll find something else to help you avoid these thoughts, like remembering him bringing you the doll.

You may learn more about how that scene in your bedroom relates to what you're feeling now. When I count from ten to one backwards, you will wake up."

When Nancy opened her eyes, I asked, "Do you recall the incident you were just telling me about?"

"No, I don't remember anything after you said that my eyes were getting heavy." I realized this scene must have had something threatening to it, since she was experiencing spontaneous amnesia again. But she looked relaxed. "I sure feel better. Did you say I wouldn't have the hallucinations anymore? I kind of think I won't."

"I just said you might be ready to give them up. If not, just remind yourself that you're not crazy. It only means you're a good hypnotic subject doing something like self-hypnosis. Sure you don't remember anything? You were talking about a baby doll with blond hair."

There was a flash of recognition. "Oh, yes. I remember being in bed. Daddy had given her to me. That was my favorite doll. She had all kinds of wonderful baby clothes. I guess he gave me the others later."

This made sense, given her father's affinity for infantile attire. Some men dress this way to gratify a sexual fetish. Other adults with dissociative disorders and childlike attitudes similar to Nancy's find such clothing a regressively soothing relief from adult roles. It was impossible to know which might be the case with Nancy's father, but obviously he had some strong affinity for diapers. Nancy thought his bizarre attire was only a function of his drinking. I assumed that it was not random but that possibly the only time he allowed himself to indulge his impulses was while intoxicated. More likely, the only time he allowed himself to be caught was when he was drunk.

This was all Nancy remembered about the doll. She had no idea how the pleasant nocturnal interlude related to her current hallucinations. I encouraged her to call me midweek if she had any more frightening hallucinations.

She did not call. The hallucinations had disappeared. By the next session, Nancy had important information about their origin. "I got to thinking that Meg would remember about the dolls 'cause she was older. I'd wanted to call her ever since Dad went in the hospital. I wasn't even sure if she knew he was there. It turned out that Mother had called. Mom told Meg that it was Meg's fault, said that the stress of her going out with a black guy had made Dad crack up. Meg hung up on her before getting all the details of what had happened to Dad, so I told her more. Then I asked her about the dolls. She remembered right away. You know what she said? 'That's what he brought us as presents when he came home from the hospital *the other time*!' I didn't know Dad had ever been in a hospital before, but he was there three months for the same thing—he was drinking. Apparently he'd stashed oversize diapers and plastic pants around the house that time, too.

"It was so great to talk to Meg. I wish I could see her. She was telling me to come visit or even spend this summer in San Diego. She told me about all the journalism internships there. I wish I didn't have to go home for the summer, but Mom—and even Dad—would be so disappointed in me if I was out there associating with Meg and her boyfriend.

"After she described the other time, I started kind of remembering. I have an image of Meg and me always hiding in some corner of the house trying to stay out of

Mom's way and asking Jimmy what kind of mood she was in. It was awful to be there with no one but Mom. I felt so much safer when Dad was home."

In this and subsequent sessions, Nancy began to tell me about abuse she had suffered at the hands of her mother. Her father did not have to go nearly as far away as a psychiatric hospital for her to be in danger. On multiple occasions he returned from work to have a "fall" of Nancy's or Meg's reported to him. He stitched cuts and tended bruises that Nancy wished he would guess the origin of, but she never dared tell him directly. Although Nancy was quite invested in her view of Jimmy as unfairly favored, she was aware that her mother at times battered him also.

When I discussed these incidents with Hunter, it turned out he knew most of them, although Nancy had presented them to him in a minimizing, self-blaming tone. I was frustrated that he hadn't shared the information, but he said he thought it better that the patient confide it herself. Nancy and I pressed on with our sessions. Her memories of the abuse were clearer and more emotional in hypnosis, but she had always had access to much of this when awake. I did not see her amnesia again until about a month later, when she arrived for a session distraught and confused.

"You look upset. What happened?"

"Rags died, my little puppy."

"How?"

"I'm not sure. I don't remember exactly. I'm so confused. She was so cute, and . . . now she's dead."

"And you don't know what happened?"

"I'm afraid to think about it."

"Were you there when she died?" I asked, still trying to get some orientation.

"I don't know; it's too terrible to remember. She was just lying there on the black linoleum of my apartment floor not moving, and she was dead. I have her covered with a blanket now. My roommate said she'd help me take her up to White Forest and bury her this afternoon after classes." Nancy was sobbing desolately.

"While you're here with me, do you want to try to remember what happened with hypnosis?" The alternative was to stay with her grief, but I didn't want to ignore whatever aspect of her pet's death had been traumatic enough to trigger Nancy's complete amnesia about it.

"Yes," Nancy replied, but she just sobbed harder. I wordlessly handed her Kleenex at regular intervals from the wooden box that sat between us.

Finally, after one round of nose blowing and eye dabbing, her sobs ceased and her eyes remained closed. She looked like she was already in trance. I was wondering whether to begin deepening procedures with staircase imagery when she spoke in a quiet, flat voice. "I think Kurt killed Rags."

"You want to tell me more?" I ventured, still unsure whether she was describing something she suspected or had witnessed.

"She had peed on the carpet while we were at the movie last night. There was a big yellow puddle that went all the way up to the rug where Kurt had laid his books. He got so mad. He started yelling, 'Bad dog!' and kicked her.

"Stop it—you're hurting her." Nancy's perspective switched to being in the scene. "Stop, don't," she pleaded.

"Keep telling me what Kurt did to Rags last night." I used the past tense to give her more distance from the scene.

"He kicked her in the ribs again and again, and then he kicked her in the head. She fell down and started jerking all over. I guess it was a seizure. Her eyes rolled way up as she thrashed around, and then she was just barely twitching . . . and then still. She wasn't breathing anymore. He killed her," she whispered.

Nancy spoke as if we were doing hypnosis, even though her trance was so far self-induced. I didn't think she needed any deepening. "You can let this terrible feeling about Rags form a bridge to take you back, looking for whether there is another place and time when you felt the same way, something that would tell you why you got so confused about what happened. Do you see another setting? Who's there? How old are you?"

"I'm in the kitchen with my family," Nancy responded immediately. "It's breakfast time. Meg leaves, I want to go with her.

" 'No young lady,' Mom says." Nancy's voice distorted into a parody of malevolence. " 'You'll stay until you've finished your bowl of cereal.'

"It's cold oatmeal. I hate it. I look over at Dad, hoping he'll say I don't have to finish, but he's busy helping Jimmy into his jacket. Jimmy doesn't have to eat cold oatmeal. I take a bit in my spoon and play with it. I roll the bowl around, pretending it will get smaller if I spin it. Oops, it spills!" Nancy sounds frightened.

" 'Terrible child.' " Nancy imitated the vicious voice

again. "She shoves me. I fall back. Ouch! The side of my head hits the table. I'm on the floor, and she kicks me in the ribs. Kicks again and again. 'I didn't mean to . . . Daddy! Daddy!' 'No, don't,' he says, 'you'll kill her.' He's pleading. He sounds so helpless, why doesn't he just *stop* her?

". . . When it's all through and she's gone, he comes over to me. 'Nancy, are you hurt, Princess?' he asks. 'Come on, I'll make everything all right.' He picks me up gently and carries me into the bathroom. He gives me one of the big white pills from the prescription bottle. They always make it stop hurting. He feels my sides. 'You might have a cracked rib. Since we can't X-ray it, we'll tape it just to make sure. You'll be as good as new.' I've stopped crying now . . ."

After I'd awakened her from the trance, Nancy speculated, "Those pills must have been codeine or something. They got rid of really bad pain. I think I had adhesive tape around my chest for a long time.

"I always thought he'd protect me if he saw. Mom seemed huge to me then, but she was actually petite— built like I am now. Dad was much larger than her. He could have stopped her in a second. I thought he didn't know. Of course any fool would have known, unless he just didn't want to face it."

She shifted her focus. "I was just like Dad. I just let Kurt kill Rags."

"It's not the same, is it? You just said your dad is larger than your mom. You're not larger than Kurt, are you? You're always telling me how big he is."

"Yes." She sounded unpersuaded.

"Does Kurt ever hit you?"

"Just a little, and it's usually my fault."

Later, when I repeated this to Hunter, he said it was more than just a little. "I've seen her with a black eye," he told me. "It's ironic; I was raised to just go out and shoot guys like him, but instead I'm making interpretations about her repetition compulsion." The lanky Texan looked unconvinced that the psychoanalytic way was an improvement over frontier justice. "Kurt is bad news. When she gets a little self-confidence, she'll drop him," he predicted.

Actually, Nancy didn't have to get more self-confidence. While she may have thought she'd done something to justify being beaten, she knew Rags didn't deserve to die. In her next session, Nancy told me that the evening after she and her roommate had returned from burying the dead puppy, Kurt dropped by.

"I don't want to see you anymore," Nancy told him. "If I hadn't been going out with you, Rags would still be alive." She was still blaming herself, even as she confronted him.

"I'll buy you a new dog," Kurt offered.

Rage had been modeled for her often enough in her life, so it was not surprising Nancy could exhibit it. "I don't want a new dog! I want a new *boyfriend*! Get out! Get *out* of here!" She took advantage of her roommate's presence to enforce the order. She also kept people around her over the next few days when walking in areas of the campus where she knew she might see Kurt. He disappeared more easily than do some violent young men. It was impossible to guess what torments may have lain behind his casual facade.

Nancy's actions after Rags's death were not unusual. Many children are able to report the first abuse of a younger sibling after having endured their own secretly for years. Many—although not enough—women leave a long-abusive partner when he begins to strike their children.

The breakup with Kurt was the first of many changes for Nancy. Most directly related was her beginning to date some of the other young men who promptly asked her out. They praised her charms and talents, which Kurt had never done. If she did not wholeheartedly believe all the new compliments, at least Nancy listened. She also began to consider not going home for the summer but instead getting a journalism internship in San Diego and living with her sister. "I think I've been avoiding Meg not just 'cause Mom and Dad are furious about her boyfriend but also because she's so outspoken about the awful parts of our childhood. Sometimes I want to pretend it was great, but I know she's right. I probably need to face it."

After Nancy had applied to several internships, we used hypnosis to practice telling her father about her plans. At this stage of treatment, she had decided to avoid her mother for a while, but she desperately wanted her father to understand her decision about the summer. The hypnotic dialogue evoked some surprising material. She imagined her father repeating things he'd said in the past criticizing Meg's interracial romance. Nancy responded, "Some people would really be prejudiced about things *you* do, but Meg never was. You could afford to be more liberal." This conversation went magnificently in imagery and pretty well in real life. Nancy's father was not likely to contradict a woman asserting herself, and he did love his "little princesses" in his own, ineffectual way. He didn't volunteer to advocate tolerance to his wife, but he did wish Nancy a good summer and told her to give his love to Meg.

Nancy came into her last therapy session to say good-bye dressed in a white cotton shift and high-heeled sandals. She touched her fingers together thoughtfully as she described the summer internship at a small women's magazine, which she'd chosen from among three offers. For months now she had been a complete nonsmoker, with her asthma well under control. It was harder to tell whether she had permanently broken free from her pattern of abusive relationships. This was a deeper issue and more difficult for hypnosis alone to transform, but she seemed to be started on an alternate course.

In retrospect, I would worry more about the abrupt switch in Nancy's therapists given what I subsequently learned about what a warm male abandoning her to the care of a woman could remind her of. Subsequent supervisors have suggested to me that you can't make progress in therapy without directly addressing transference—how the patient feels about the therapist, reminders of significant others from the past, and termination issues from previous therapy. Fortunately, the nature of therapy seems to be more forgiving than that. It is possible for the therapist to make mistakes, pick up only a few of the myriad threads of someone's life, and still lend the patient the courage to change.

If Nancy projected me, a woman only four years older

than herself, into any slot in her family constellation, I probably reminded her more of her older sister, Meg, than of her mother. Perhaps the shift from Hunter to me helped move Nancy's focus away from her father and the vain fantasy that he would rescue her so that she could begin to play the role of a competent adult.

2

The Assailant and the Baby-sitter

Dolores picked up the steel butcher knife from the kitchen counter and shifted it experimentally between her veined, callused hands, settling on a downward grip with the left. She advanced slowly toward the young man seated with his back to her at the old wooden table. Her dark eyes and lined face were expressionless as she stopped behind him and raised the knife. Standing at the stove, a young woman screamed, "God, what . . . *Dave!*" The young man shot an astonished look over his shoulder and leapt sideways out of the chair. The knife blade flashed down through the space he had just occupied. Dolores slowly raised the knife again.

"Mother, stop it! What's wrong with you?" Dave howled as she backed him into the living room, knocking the modest but neat furnishings into disarray.

The slight, middle-aged woman's movements quickened, and her blank expression was replaced by a malicious glare. "I'll kill you, I'll kill you, I'll kill you!" Dolores rasped as she charged him.

Dave fled out of the living room, down the hall, and slammed his bedroom door shut. He flipped the lock a moment before his mother arrived. She plunged the knife into the door with all the force in her small, wiry frame. The old wood cracked and splintered, allowing the knife to penetrate two inches into the room. Dolores thrust again and again until the blade pierced up to the hilt and lodged in the wood. She continued to pound both knife and door, bloodying her fists on the jagged wood. "I'll kill you," she repeated in the same eerie voice.

Dave's sister, Frances, had followed them into the hallway. Throughout the attack, she implored her mother to stop but grabbed her arm only after the knife jammed in the door. Dolores made no move to attack Frances, nor did she respond to her touch. Perhaps she did not even perceive her daughter. From inside the bedroom, Dave telephoned the police.

By the time two officers arrived, Dolores was sitting slumped on the bare hall floor in a semistuporous state. They had trouble getting her to speak. When she did, "I don't know" and "I didn't" were her only responses to their many questions. Two weeks before I was to meet her, Dolores Travers was involuntarily committed to my medical school's locked psychiatric unit for a ten-day evaluation.

"No, there was no argument, no one was even talking right before I saw her coming at Dave. Just a half hour earlier, she'd been asking him nicely how work was. . . . No, she's never seen a psychiatrist. There was never any reason to. Mom was always so sweet. She never raised a hand to us when we were growing up." Frances did most of the talking in the admissions interview. Dave answered questions directly related to him. No, he wasn't considering pressing assault charges. Dolores sat silently, staring at the floor.

"She wasn't drinking today. . . . Yeah, she does sometimes drink too much, but she's still real friendly, kinda fun when she's drunk. . . . No, she's never been in trouble with the law. . . . Yes, I'm sure. We've lived with her all but two years. Five years ago she moved to New York with just Angie, who was the only little one then. After she got pregnant with Jimmy, she came home. Even during the time she was back East, we used to talk to her on the phone. There was never any problem."

A portrait emerged of a woman who had worked hard, partied hard, and made the best of a rough existence. Dolores had been in two short marriages and dozens of short jobs. She'd given birth to seven children, the first when she was fifteen, the last when she was forty-four. The children had worked from their early teens, often as janitors—Frances currently scrubbed and polished the floors of the very hospital to which her mother was being admitted. Besides Dave and Frances, the youngest—Angie and Tommy—lived at home with Dolores. The middle three children were on their own in other cities but kept in close touch. They were a loyal clan and were rallying to their mother's support—even the son she'd just tried to stab.

Dolores didn't say a word during the admissions process. Her only reaction was at the end of the interview, when a nurse came to escort her to her room. The R.N. reached for Dolores's cigarettes, explaining that no smoking was allowed in the bedrooms. Cigarettes were kept in the nursing station, to be handed out only for assigned smoking times in the dayroom. Dolores clutched the pack tightly. The nurse tried coaxing but eventually yanked hard against her patient's resistance. "No, mine!" Dolores wailed as they were pried out of her hands. Now Dolores looked more confused than threatening. Reverting to silence, she allowed herself to be led off down the wide green-gray corridor.

The night admissions officer called Medical Records to request charts of any previous in- or outpatient treatment Dolores might have received. This was routine, but the records for her medical outpatient visits were not easily located. They never arrived during her ten-day stay.

However, the next morning, her inpatient record from two years earlier was in the mailbox of Dr. Roger Willis, the young resident assigned to Dolores's case. Her one previous hospital stay, two years earlier, had been on a medical unit. The circumstances were quite different from her present psychiatric admission, but equally mysterious. They offered one possible explanation for her bizarre behavior of the previous night.

The Emergency Room note read:

5/14/76—Forty-six-year-old divorced white female admitted unconscious due to head trauma. Skull X

rays negative for current fracture, healed 8-inch
fracture line on left side from 5 years of age. EEG
shows diffuse slowing. CAT scan indicates severe
concussion. Monitor in Intensive Care.

The day before this 1976 medical admission, a broad-
shouldered, good-looking man in his fifties had rung the
bell of the dilapidated two-story wooden house Dolores
occupied with her children. He told Frances and Dave that
he was Dolores's husband. They indicated they found this
implausible and said they were her grown children. He indicated he found *that* implausible. They called their
mother to the door. Dolores looked bewildered. "I've
never seen you before in my life," they heard her tell the
visitor.

"Dolly," he said, using a nickname her children had
never heard her use, "I want us to get back together. You
just took off and never gave me a chance to apologize."
Their mother was docile, not turning on the flirtatious
charm Frances and Dave usually observed when Mom
was with a man. Dolores continued to deny knowing the
visitor, much less being married to him. However, they
heard him persuading her that he should return the next
day.

The following afternoon, Dave and Frances were at
work and Angie was at school. Dolores had taken Baby
Tommy out on the second-floor porch overlooking their
small, wooded backyard. It was a crisp spring day. No
one—children, doctors, police—ever learned what tran-
spired during that second visit, or even for sure that the
man returned. Hours later, when Dave came home from
work, he found Dolores unconscious on the lawn beneath

the deck, broken pieces of rotten porch railing scattered in an arc around her. On her chest sat Tommy, howling but unharmed except for minor bruises. This time, too, Dave made the emergency call.

Dolores was rushed to the hospital. She did not regain consciousness until the next day. Then she was groggy and confused, suffering from severe postconcussion syndrome. Usually a head injury of this severity causes something called retrograde amnesia—forgetfulness of events before the blow. During the period of unconsciousness, the chemical messenger acetylcholine, which converts fragile short-term memory traces into long-term storage, is shut off, and the information is lost forever. This is the same reason we lose so many of our dreams if we don't wake up immediately after them.

However, Dolores had forgotten more than a few hours. She didn't remember any of the staff in the hospital, even though the same nurses came into her room many times each shift. This inability to form new memories suggested potential brain damage, but it was hard to be sure until the swelling of her concussion cleared.

Police investigated the incident as a possible assault, but the descriptions—"kind of nice-looking, maybe fifty-five" and "Dolly's husband"—were not sufficient clues to track her male visitor down. The railing was rotted enough that leaning hard might have caused it to give way. It was not certain that Dolores had been thrown against it.

Over the next week, Dolores's confusion cleared a bit. However, her retrograde amnesia for the hours before the fall was permanent. The detective in charge closed the case, unable to rule out an accident. The stranger never reappeared.

Two years later on the psychiatric unit, Dolores behaved like someone with brain damage. She was withdrawn, showed no emotion, answered questions in monosyllables, and remembered little. Her only spontaneous conversation revolved around when she could smoke. Five minutes into the hourlong wait between smoking times, she asked the nurses, "Do you have a cigarette? Do you have a match?" She appeared to watch TV, but when another patient would change the channel abruptly, she was not part of the general uproar that the staff had to negotiate. She gazed at the new show as steadily as she had at the previous one.

A neuropsychologist had given her intelligence tests. His report stated mostly the obvious:

48-year-old right-handed female scores 86 on IQ test, with fund of current information subnormal— i.e., cannot name current president of the United States. Fails single-digit addition and subtraction. Consistent with organic brain damage due to 1976 head trauma and/or 35-year history of alcohol abuse.

Despite this report, Frances, who visited multiple times on her hospital breaks, and Dave, who came most evenings, continued to describe their mother as a lively, sharp person—not just before the fall from the porch but, strangely, since, flouting the nurses' and doctor's observations.

Frances also told Dr. Willis the story of Dolores's childhood. No one knew who her biological parents were or what their home life had been like, but something must have gone terribly wrong. As a toddler, Dolores had been placed in an institution that housed orphaned and abandoned children together with mentally retarded and psychotic adults. "Mom hated the place *real* bad, but she never really talked about what happened there," Frances said. Dolores had lived there until the age of thirteen, when she ran away and began to work.

The medical chart revealed an even more sinister version of the story. Doctors examining Dolores during her two hospitalizations had found multiple fractures dating back to childhood—including the large left skull fracture noted in the ER report and a ruptured eardrum on the same side, which rendered her deaf in that ear. Because of the rapid rate of bone growth in childhood, doctors could date these injuries to age five. Dolores's body bore many other scars from cuts and burns a bit later, which were harder to date exactly but had all been sustained before age ten.

Dr. Willis questioned the Hieronymus Bosch–like image that Frances's description of the institution and the scars conjured up. However, when he asked the oldest psychiatrist in the department if orphanages and insane asylums had ever been combined, he was told that such joint institutions, with little supervision and frequent violence, did exist during the thirties in the rural West. So this horror story probably was childhood for his patient.

The nurses on the unit couldn't tell Dr. Willis much of interest about Dolores. They were usually occupied with more disruptive patients. One young woman frequently screamed in alarm as she hallucinated snakes writhing on the floor. She jumped up on furniture or tried to climb the drapes, pulling them down. A gaunt young man periodically heard a voice commanding him to remove his clothing. He assaulted anyone who attempted to dissuade him. Several times a day, the naked man was locked in the padded seclusion room, banging on the steel door and cursing. Dolores made no trouble, so she got little of the overburdened staff's attention.

Dr. Willis was struck by two things in her chart. First, there was the story of the stranger-husband and the fall. The chart also contained scans of Dolores's brain showing no obvious lasting structural damage. That is often the case: many brain injuries are at the cellular level, not visible even to modern technology. However, Dr. Willis was more intrigued by the other possible implication. In the medical school's hypnosis course, which he was currently taking, he had learned that some amnesias are psychogenic, or emotionally caused, and therefore potentially reversible. Hypnosis is the most powerful treatment for psychogenic amnesia. Possibly foremost in his awareness, however, was that he had a homework assignment to practice hypnotizing two patients that week. Dolores certainly seemed like an uncritical audience, not likely to laugh at him or mention his failure to others if he botched an induction. In the haphazard manner that things sometimes happen in teaching hospitals, six days into Dolores Travers's stay, Dr. Willis decided to put her in a trance and regress her to the day she fell from the porch.

He took her into the quietest of the small interview rooms off the hospital corridor—the one farthest from the seclusion room that housed the naked screamer. It lacked the recliner or couch that would have been ideal for a hypnotic induction, so each sat in one of the sculpted plastic chairs. Dr. Willis had the instruction sheet for the "arm levitation" induction assigned for this week folded in front of him. He had memorized enough that he wouldn't be reading, but it was comforting to have the paper with him, just in case. Dolores asked if he had a cigarette. He told her no: smoking time was later.

Dr. Willis asked Dolores to put her hands in her lap, to watch them, and to notice which one of them got lighter. He had to repeat the suggestion for positioning her hands before she followed it. At first she glanced from side to side, as if looking for a pack of Marlboros or matches. However, as he continued to talk about staring, her gaze became fixed. He spoke more about lightness. Her left hand began to twitch. The tips of her fingers lifted a bit.

This was Dr. Willis's first arm levitation, and it was happening just like the demonstration in class. He was so excited and nervous that he realized he didn't know what came next. He glanced surreptitiously at the paper before him—ah yes, the balloon. He told Dolores that her hand would become lighter and lighter, as light as air; that it would lift as if a balloon were attached to her wrist. He repeated these things slowly, trying to imitate the soothing tone of his hypnosis instructor. Indeed, Dolores's whole hand and arm started to rise. He told her that the hand would come toward her face and that, when it did, her eyes would close and she would be deeply asleep. This happened. Dolores appeared to be in a trance.

He asked her to imagine herself on the porch that day. "It's sunny; you're holding Baby Tommy. Do you see the man who says he's your husband there?"

"No, I don't see anything," Dolores said.

"Can you see the porch, the yard?"

"I don't see anything," Dolores repeated. Her voice sounded crisp, certain. At least she wasn't asking for cigarettes.

Dr. Willis tried suggesting things associated with that day several times more. Dolores continued to report no imagery, but she was remarkably attentive. After a few minutes, Dr. Willis counted backwards with a wake-up suggestion. Dolores opened her eyes. She was her same uncommunicative self as before the trance. The session had been a complete failure in terms of memory recovery. However, Dolores did seem to have been hypnotized. Dr. Willis was still at such an early stage in his practice that he didn't quite expect anyone to respond to his inductions. More significant, he'd been taught that people with disoriented organic brain damage were rarely hypnotizable.

The next step in Dolores's evaluation was for the psychiatric unit to hold a case conference to formulate her treatment plan. The commitment for observation would expire soon. If they thought she was still "a clear and present danger to self or others," as the legal criteria read, they needed time to request a ninety-day commitment for treatment.

Often the case conferences were forums for lengthy, abstract speculation about the patient's psychodynamics. The woman who hallucinated snakes provoked a lively debate between advocates of classic Freudian phallic symbolism and those favoring Jungian serpents as totems for the underworld, poison, death.

However, when patients were judged to be severely

brain-damaged, discussion was usually shorter and more practical: how much caretaking the person needed, techniques to compensate for lost memory, such as strategic placements of reminder notes. There was less opportunity to show off in these presentations on organic lesions but also less possibility for the humiliations visited on trainees judged not to have understood their patients' psychodynamics.

Because Dolores's case was not one of the more sensational, a smaller group than usual attended. The chief psychiatrist for the ward presided. Dr. Willis and the other three psychiatry residents were there, along with the two nurses who worked most with Dolores. They spread out around a conference table that accommodated up to twenty. Dr. Willis summarized the information in twenty minutes. The Chief and one favored resident jumped in as usual, asking for historical details that Dr. Willis had not addressed. For once he answered these volleys comfortably, because he could easily make the case that the answers to their queries could not be obtained from this patient.

He did broach two awkward inconsistencies with the brain-damaged portrait: her children described Dolores as much more functional than she'd ever been on the ward, and she was hypnotizable. The Chief dismissed the former as her children covering for her because they were unable to face her impairment. Dr. Willis was convinced that Frances and Dave were the type who could face just about anything head-on, but he kept this thought to himself. In these meetings it was ironic to watch the people with the least knowledge of a patient work up much more confident formulations than those who actually knew the patient. However, it would have been dangerous to one's career for a mere trainee or nurse to try to derail one of these fantasy trains once it worked up steam.

The Chief and the favored resident debated the source of Dave and Frances's denial: the dependent need for a strong parent or guilt over having unconsciously wished for Dolores's downfall. Dr. Willis listened quietly and nodded mechanically at the Chief's side of the dialogue.

As to Dolores's capacity for hypnosis, the Chief ridiculed the idea that amnesia following a head trauma would be due to anything but the temporary shutdown of acetylcholine release. Dr. Willis was also criticized because if the patient had actually repressed something, pushing to recover the memory so rapidly with no therapeutic rapport established could be quite upsetting to the patient. The favored resident began to disparage any use of hypnosis with the brain-damaged, but the Chief had registered the fact that Dolores was described as more lucid in the trance state. He thought it might calm her agitation. No one had any better therapy ideas, and it was anathema simply to decide that a patient couldn't benefit from psychotherapy. The consensus was to refer Dolores for hypnotherapy.

Treatment would be done on an outpatient basis. With no further incidents of violence, Dolores's danger potential was neither "clear" nor "present." No one felt very safe about her either, but you couldn't hold a patient just because she might possibly attack someone again in two years. There was a brief discussion of whether the stabbing attempt could have been caused by a seizure in the temporal lobe. This occasional result of head trauma can create rage in the absence of provocation, or violence in the absence of anger. However, repeated EEGs showed no abnormal brain waves. It was decided there was no sense starting Dolores on medication unless the episode was repeated. So she was given a referral for hypnotherapy, instructions for a follow-up EEG in three months, and permission to leave when the ten-day involuntary commitment expired.

I was the only trainee doing hypnotherapy in the medical school's outpatient clinic. Although I was sitting in on the course Dr. Willis was taking, I had been using hypnosis for three years since I had begun working with Nancy—first at my graduate school practicum, now at my Colorado internship. Thus Dolores's inpatient chart arrived in my box. I read through the unencouraging account of her present state. Then I talked to her inpatient team and got the rest of the gloomy details I've just described. The referral bordered on what we called a "dump"—sending an impossible patient to someone not in a position to refuse. However, I was intrigued by the same strange details that had caught Dr. Willis's attention.

Frances called later that week to schedule her mother's appointment. She sounded pleasant but worried: "Maybe hypnosis will help her. I don't think being in the hospital did." She explained that her mother probably wouldn't come unless she brought her, so we made the appointment for Frances's day off, the following Wednesday.

Tuesday evening, I stopped Dr. Willis after the hypnosis seminar. "I have my first appointment with Dolores tomorrow. Any last-minute additions to what you've told me?"

"There's something weird about hypnosis with her. She's *present* and, well, *smarter.*" Something in Dr. Willis's voice suggested that there was more he wanted to convey, but words failed him.

The next morning, Frances and Dolores arrived together. They were both small, wiry women with dark coloring and strong bone structure. They could have been Native American except each had a black cloud of curls around her face, Dolores's almost certainly dyed.

Frances introduced herself warmly. She wore heavy mascara and iridescent green eye shadow. This gave her a coarse look, but her manner was fresh and sweet. Dolores wore no makeup on her lined, drawn face. Her expression was as bland as the chart described, and she did not speak.

"I have to run down to Housekeeping to get my paycheck," Frances told me, "but I'll be back to pick her up. Mother, the doctor's going to talk to you for an hour, then we'll go on to the store." She was gone. I felt strange being left with Dolores still standing in my doorway, not yet having spoken.

"Come in. Have a seat." I gestured to a high-backed armchair. To my relief, Dolores sat down.

"Do you have a cigarette?" Her voice was flat. She scanned the bookshelf as if expecting a pack there. Instead, there was a large NO SMOKING sign. I'd grown less tolerant of the habit in the three years since I'd seen Nancy. The sign did not seem to register.

"No, I don't have any. I'm the hypnotherapist your other doctors wanted you to see. Did they talk to you about that?"

She didn't answer but rummaged through her purse

and, to my dismay, fished out a pack of Marlboros. "I'd rather you didn't smoke here; the ventilation's not so good," I told her.

"Do you have a match?" I couldn't tell if she didn't hear, didn't understand me, or was choosing to ignore what I said.

"No, I don't." She began to search her handbag. I weighed whether to resist further if she started to light up. Fortunately, there were no matches in her purse.

"I wanted to hypnotize you today like Dr. Willis did. Do you remember that?"

Dolores looked confused. "No," she said warily.

"Do you remember Dr. Willis?" I asked.

She hesitated. "No." It was now six days since her hospital stay. I was doubtful whether anything could help this woman. I would certainly not have been pursuing hypnosis except for Dr. Willis's report.

"I'd be asking you to relax and talking to you about sleep. Then we'd just see how you felt once you were in hypnosis. Would that be all right with you?" I was indeed simply planning to explore what she was like in a trance, not to go chasing after memories of accidents or assaults. I did not yet have the rapport or understanding of her that I'd had with Nancy when I began probing her traumatic memories.

"Okay," Dolores said flatly. Did this constitute informed consent? It was hard to tell how much she comprehended. Perhaps hypnosis was the only thing likely to help. Furthermore, it was painful to interact with her any other way.

"Let me know any time you want to stop," I began cautiously. "What I'd like you to do first is to put your hands in your lap." Arm levitation is not the induction I usually start with. The eye closure I used with Nancy is what I initially try unless the person has vision problems. However, if a patient has had a good experience with hypnosis in the past, it is useful to build on that. It may not have mattered much with Dolores, who had no conscious memory of Dr. Willis's induction, but I figured there was no reason to tamper with success.

"Stare at your hands and let your body begin to relax. As you stare at them, you will notice one of your hands beginning to get lighter, maybe just barely at first. The fingertips will begin to lift up." Her left hand twitched, and three fingers moved off her lap.

"As you keep relaxing your body and listening to my voice, you will find the hand getting lighter and lighter. It feels like a balloon is tied to your wrist, pulling your arm up and up." I repeated this several times. Her hand lifted. Her whole left arm began to float as I had suggested. Her fingers slowly closed inward—I had not suggested this.

I felt a chill as I realized how closely the left arm raised with the blank gaze replicated the attempted stabbing. I glanced quickly around the office as Dolores had earlier when looking for cigarettes. My scissors sitting in the pencil tray were fairly blunt, but I still wished I had stashed them in a drawer. This was definitely not the induction I would have chosen, but, again, it had gone well for Dr. Willis.

"You can let the fingers of your hand relax as it gradually moves toward your face. When the hand touches your face, your eyes will close and you can go into a deep sleep." This happened. Dolores appeared to be hypnotized again. My apprehension passed.

"You can let your arm move back down. Gradually, normal weight will return to your arm. The balloon is gone, and your hand can rest in your lap again. Very good. Now that you're so relaxed, I want you to think about the name 'Dr. Willis' again. Do you know who that is now?"

"No, I don't." This was the first complete sentence I'd heard from her that didn't have to do with cigarettes, and she'd spoken in a clear voice.

"Try thinking of the name 'Dr. Willis' and see if a face comes to mind. Do you see a face?"

"No, I don't see anything."

I decided to test some of her other deficits since I was getting nowhere with her memory for six days ago. "I want to ask you to add and subtract some numbers and tell me the answers. The first is two plus two. Can you tell me what that equals?"

"Two plus two is four." No great feat, except that she hadn't been able to do it a week ago for the neuropsychologist.

"And three plus five?"

"Eight." Her head had rotated slightly, moving her right ear—the good one—closer to me. This reinforced my impression that she hadn't been trying to listen much outside of trance.

"And nine minus two—what does that equal?"

"Seven." Dolores followed suggestions, and hypnosis apparently made her less aware of everyday concerns such as cigarettes. However, she wasn't the typical hypnotized subject. Most people's facial muscles relax in hypnosis. Hers gained tone; her jaw no longer drooped. Her eyes were closed, but in every other way she appeared more attentive than before.

After a few more tests of her improved cognition, I suggested that Dolores wake up as I counted backwards from ten to one. As soon as her eyes opened, the cigarette refrain began. I stepped into the hallway and invited Frances to join us.

"Were you hypnotized, Mom?" Frances asked.

"Do you have a match?" Dolores had found her Marlboros.

"It says 'No Smoking,' Mom. Wait till we get outside." Frances turned back to me. "Was she hypnotized?"

"I think so. She certainly seems clearer after I do a hypnotic induction. Next week I want to age-regress her a little way, back to when she was happy and functioning well, before the incident with Dave. Could you tell me something like that, a happy time before she went into the hospital?"

"Just any time that was good?"

"Yes."

"Well, I keep thinking how that very morning everything was real nice. We were in the kitchen eating breakfast. The morning news was on. They were saying Pat Schroeder was reelected, and Mom cheered 'cause that's her candidate. Angie came in and wanted help making decorations for her school party. Mom showed her how to fold the construction paper over and over and cut in a circle. That makes pretty flowers real easy. Everything was just happy and normal."

The best way to imagine Dolores being a lively, loving person was to look at Frances. Dolores was easier to like if I thought of Frances as a younger version of her. Frances's warmth and cheer probably mirrored her mother's past kindness to her.

"Dolores, do you remember that morning Frances is describing?" I asked.

"No," she answered hesitantly. Again, I doubted if she'd even been listening.

As I ushered them toward the door, I said, "Next week we'll try to get you in touch with that memory and see if it carries over into how you feel after. How does that sound?"

"Okay," Dolores responded flatly and shuffled out without further comment.

"Good-bye, thanks." Frances smiled. "She'll see you next week."

That Friday I met with my supervisor, Dr. Julia Olson. Just as in graduate school, I was being supervised by someone who didn't do hypnosis herself. However, Dr. Olson had extensive experience with brain damage. She looked carefully through Dolores's inpatient record.

"It certainly sounds like severe impairment from her head injury," she told me. "And long-term alcohol damage can show up at about this age; it might be contributing, too. But her level of functioning changes a lot. You want to be thinking about whether these fluctuations are the natural course of the brain damage or whether she exaggerates her defects to get taken care of. Since she's more coherent in hypnosis, I'd continue that for now."

When she asked if I had Dolores's outpatient medical record, I was reminded that it had never been delivered to either the inpatient unit or my office. I phoned the records librarian again and requested that she begin a formal missing record search. She agreed to but told me it was very likely lost for good. I hoped not; I needed every bit of information I could get.

The following Wednesday at two, Dolores was outside my office. I looked around, but there was no sign of anyone else.

"Did Frances bring you?" I asked.

"No."

I wasn't sure whether to believe her. "How did you get here?"

Dolores looked uncertain and began to fumble in her purse. "Do you have a cigarette?"

"No." God, she was uncomfortable to be with.

"Today we were going to do hypnosis again. Do you remember being hypnotized last week?"

"No."

"Do you remember *me* from last week?"

"No." She was still looking through the handbag.

"I'm Deirdre Barrett. I'm your outpatient therapist. Today I'd like to hypnotize you and have you think about some happy times."

"Okay." This time she didn't seem to have the Marlboros in the purse.

I repeated the arm levitation induction, and she went into trance as easily as before.

"I want you to feel yourself beginning to move back in time, as if the pages of a calendar were flipping backwards, just a little way." I usually don't have an exact target date, but it had been easy to look up the day of her admission. "You can move back until you stop at the morning of November third. It's a Wednesday, breakfast time. The TV's on, and the announcer is talking about

Representative Schroeder winning the election. Dave and Frances are there; can you see them?"

"No, I don't see anything."

"Well, maybe you could focus on when Angie walked in holding colored construction paper for her decorations. If you think about that, can you see her?"

"No, I don't see anything."

Maybe she just didn't have as much visual imagery as most people. I quit asking about "seeing" things. "Do you remember helping Angie cut out flowers?"

"No, I don't remember."

I switched my line of questioning. "Do you know my name?"

"No, I don't." Dolores had no more memory now than when she was awake, but she was speaking in complete sentences.

Then I thought to ask, "How did you get here today?"

"I took the bus."

"Did Frances ride the bus with you?"

"No. She told me the bus number to transfer to."

"How are you getting home?"

"I'm taking bus eighteen to the grocery. Then bus twenty-four home."

"How did you find my office if you didn't remember my name?"

"I looked for Dr. Barrett on the third floor." She didn't seem to connect this with the person she was talking to. I continued to question Dolores for most of the hour. She could tell me many mundane details of what she'd done the last week that represented better functioning than I or the inpatient ward had observed directly. However, her remote memory remained inaccessible.

This time I suggested that when she woke up she could still remember how she got to my office and be able to talk to me about it. I counted backwards to one.

"Do you have a cigarette?"

"No. Do you remember what you just told me about coming here?"

"No."

I was at a loss for what to do next, but it was almost time for Dolores to go anyway. "Do you know how to get home?" I asked with concern.

She hesitated. "Bus," she replied warily. As I watched her trudge down the hall, I began to question the value of trying to improve her behavior or memory in my office when she seemed to do better everywhere else anyway.

Dolores missed her next appointment. When I telephoned her house late that afternoon, Frances answered. "Yeah, I know. I'm real sorry. She did fine with the bus last week, but I guess I should write down the numbers for her again. She'll be there next time. Thanks a lot for calling."

The following Wednesday, Dolores hadn't shown up by ten minutes after two. To pass the time, I began to leaf through her inpatient chart, looking at all its oddities and contradictions. Her children said she held the knife in her left hand. The neuropsychology note read "right-handed" woman. Neuropsychologists routinely have patients pick up objects, write, draw—observing whether these all occur with the same hand as they do for the 90 percent of the population who are right-handed and the 8 percent who are left-handed. Only 2 percent of people are ambidextrous, with one hand dominant for tasks such as writing and the other for functions that require strength. Ambidexterity often indicates that language and motor centers have developed on opposite sides of the brain. These patterns are usually set by age five. Occasionally, brain damage can shift the established handedness. However, Dolores's testing revealed no evidence of ambidexterity, only the assault account did.

The neuropsychologist also reported Dolores could not name the current President; Frances said her mother wanted Pat Schroeder reelected to Congress. A man claimed to be her husband; Dolores insisted she had never met him.

At twenty-five past two, it was clear to me that Dolores was not coming. My four o'clock appointment was open. I had been taught not to pursue a client who was genuinely hesitant or might be gratifying a desire to control the therapy by getting extra attention. However, structure and allowances for a brain-damaged person with memory difficulties were acceptable. As Dr. Olson had pointed out, it was hard to tell how much each was responsible for Dolores's behavior. I decided to give her the benefit of the doubt. A call now with a reminder and bus directions might get her in to see me in my free hour.

I flipped back through the chart to the pink data sheet with her home phone number and dialed. On the third ring, a cheerful teenage voice answered. "Hello?"

Was one of the middle children visiting? The accent and intonation were enough like Frances's to belong to a younger sister. Curious, I asked only "May I please speak to Dolores Travers?"

"She can't come to the phone right now." Still cheerful but terse, no explanation or offer to take a message.

"Is she home?" I asked, beginning to feel intrusive but wanting a little more information out of this call.

"Yes, but she won't come to the phone." A nervous giggle, more embarrassed than annoyed with my persistence.

"I'm calling from the Medical Center. She had a two o'clock appointment with me that she's missed," I said, careful to avoid a mention of psychiatry. "I was calling to see if she wanted to reschedule it."

"Oh, you're her shrink? I knew she had an appointment today, but she just won't get out of bed lately. She curls up in a ball on her side and pulls the covers way over her head. Stays like that all day. She won't talk to me. I never see her move. I take her a tray with iced tea and a sandwich at lunchtime and leave it on the night table. Eventually it's gone, but she doesn't stick her head out while I'm in there. She's sure not going to come to the phone." Another giggle. Maybe she was nervous talking about this, but really it sounded more like the girl found it funny and wasn't concerned.

"You're probably right, but would you just try calling her to the phone? Tell her Deirdre Barrett would like to talk to her about when she could come in." I knew this was a long shot: Dolores had not remembered me from one session to the next, much less remembered me fondly—but so far she had talked to me. I didn't know if this girl might be part of the reason for her withdrawal.

"Okay, but I'm telling you she won't come." I heard footsteps recede and muffled phrases about "Dr. Barrett on the phone" and "Get up!" but in a minute my informant was back. "Unh-unhhh. I told her you wanted to talk to her, but she didn't move a muscle."

I finally asked, "Who am I speaking to?"

"I'm the baby-sitter. I take care of Tommy when Frances and Dave are at work. And Angie when she gets home from school." I was glad to hear that Frances and Dave had decided this was necessary. I had worried about Dolores's caretaking of the young children after the assault on Dave, and obviously even more now that she was so immobile. This girl was probably good with the kids. She sounded very sweet, just unaware of the severity of the behavior she was describing—whether it was psychological or organic in nature.

"Okay, thank you very much. Could you tell Frances that Dolores missed her appointment and I'd like her to call me at the hospital tomorrow?" I left the number and signed off.

After seeing my three o'clock patient, I still had the four o'clock hour free. I headed to the basement of the psychiatry building, where vending machines with sodas, chips, and Twinkies provided the quickest calories available to tired staff who didn't want to cross the street to the main cafeteria.

There in the windowless, low-ceilinged room, vigorously scrubbing up half-dried Coke off the old linoleum, was Frances. We were alone with the soft hum of the machines.

"Your mother missed her appointment today. I wanted to talk to you about rescheduling it."

"Yeah, I know, but I don't think I can get her to come. She only gets places when I take her, or at least put her on the bus." She kept scrubbing the floor energetically. Matter-of-factly, with no trace of bitterness or even tiredness, she told me: "I've just started to work overtime, two extra shifts. We need the money with her not having a job anymore."

"But she really ought to be in therapy."

Having eradicated the last traces of the sticky spill, Frances leaned back on her mop. "I just don't think we can. Besides, she's better."

Better? "Uhhh . . . that was the other thing I wanted to talk with you about. The baby-sitter told me she's spending all day in bed in a fetal position with the covers over her head."

Frances looked baffled.

"What baby-sitter?"

"The girl who watches Angie and Tommy. I talked to her when I called your house today."

"There's never anyone at home during the day with the little ones but Mother."

I stared in complete confusion. I didn't think Frances would lie to cover up her mother's being worse. Could Dolores have hired a sitter without Frances and Dave knowing?

Frances mistook my stare for one of comprehension rather than bewilderment. She gazed at me unblinkingly, smiled slightly, and nodded—as if to say, "Yeah, you're finally getting it." My shock produced a sense of slow motion as I watched her turn on her heels and walk out of the room. The gray mop trailed behind her as she disappeared into the service elevator.

The next morning there was a hospital file sitting in my box, "Outpatient Record: Dolores Travers." Ironic timing. I didn't really expect any medical notes would illuminate my dilemma. However, Dolores was certainly on my mind. So, to focus some of my nervous energy, I opened the folder and began to read. Outpatient charts are slow going because, except for lab reports, entries are handwritten by physicians in telegraphic, semilegible scrawls. Inpatient charts are easier because intake and discharge notes are typed, and many notes are written by nurses in schoolbook-perfect script. This chart atypically consisted of terse Emergency Room notes:

> 4/16/71 ER NOTE: 41-yr.-old white married female complains of sudden deafness and pain in left ear. Auditory tests confirm complete lack of perception for all frequency ranges. No eardrum visualizable w/ otoscope. Referred rush to Ear/Nose/Throat clinic.

Huh? She'd been deaf in that ear since age five. But the ER physician didn't know that. And, somehow, neither did Dolores. I read with increasing astonishment.

> 4/16/71 E/N/T CLINIC NOTE: Patient in pain and distraught over hearing loss. Left eardrum entirely absent, significant scar tissue inside ear. Skull X ray shows healed childhood fracture contiguous to ear. Patient was told she could not have been hearing with left ear for decades. At this, she became confused, departed clinic refusing further evaluation of current pain.

> 8/5/73 ER NOTE: 43-yr.-old divorced white female reports she woke up this morning with severe pain

and no hearing in left ear. Tests confirm deafness in
all frequency ranges. Eardrum not visible on initial
exam. Rush refer to E/N/T.

8/5/73 E/N/T CLINIC NOTE: Patient experiencing
total deafness in left ear. Ear painful upon exam.
Scar tissue around ruptured eardrum. Skull fracture on left dates to age 5. Patient was informed of
findings, left the clinic appearing disoriented.

I began to skim. The chart entries repeated like this. The
only variation was that on two of her seven visits, the
Emergency Room physician read the old chart shortly after Dolores's arrival, aborting the series of tests and X rays.

In 1978 multiple personality disorder was not well known.
Only a handful of cases had been published in the professional literature. Actually, the condition had received
more attention in the popular press, with the books *The
Three Faces of Eve* and *Sybil*. The former, published in 1957,
oversimplified the syndrome greatly—a few personalities
who readily announce themselves, an instantaneous cure
after remembering one traumatic incident. As I mentioned
in the introduction, a 1989 autobiography by the real "Eve,"
Christine Costner Sizemore, was to reveal that she was not
at all cured by the time of her first therapist's book. She had
twenty-two personalities and a series of childhood traumas,
and her integration involved lengthy treatment with another therapist. At the time I saw Dolores, the 1974 *Sybil*
was the most detailed and representative book available—
it described many "alter" personalities who were reticent

about revealing themselves, long-term abuse creating the disorder, long-term therapy resolving it.

Before I ever saw Dolores, I knew she had amnesia for episodes of uncharacteristic behavior, someone who knew her by another name, alternating handedness, and a history of horrific childhood trauma. Today, if someone was referred to me with those characteristics, multiple personality would be the first thing I'd think of, well ahead of temporal lobe epilepsy or faking illness. However, my internship year it took talking to the "baby-sitter" and reading the accounts of Dolores reliving the ruptured eardrum to suspect this diagnosis. The "baby-sitter" was more organized than the behavior of a temporal lobe epilepsy patient, and the deafness routine would be pointless to fake.

By the time of my meeting with my supervisor, two days after I'd read the old chart, I had decided the diagnosis fit perfectly. I told Dr. Olson of my call to the house, my encounter with Frances, and the arrival of the old medical chart. "I think she has multiple personality," I said.

I was lucky to have a supervisor with a relatively open mind on the matter. "That could be; it would explain a lot. Multiple personality is a very rare diagnosis. I've certainly never seen one. I don't know much about it. I'm not even sure if it's real, but she does rather sound like she might have it."

I've since heard many stories of beginning therapists ridiculed out of this diagnosis. It's unusual for a supervisor simply to admit he or she doesn't know something. At that time there were a lot of teachers who "knew" the disorder didn't exist, "knew" it was so rare their student couldn't be seeing one, or "knew" a particular patient must be faking.

Despite my relief about Dr. Olson's receptivity to my formulation, I felt I had bungled things completely by not arriving at it earlier. If only I had gotten the chart sooner. If only I had used hypnosis to ask to speak to "Dolly." The only consolation was that everyone else had missed it, too. I was hoping for advice on how to regroup, get Frances to tell me what more she seemed to know of her mother's dissociation, and persuade Dolores to come back to the outpatient clinic. At least I knew hypnosis was the best mode for treating multiple personality.

"How do I get her back in?" This, Dr. Olson did have a strong opinion about.

"You don't. You've tried enough. This patient hasn't expressed any wish for psychotherapy. First she was court-ordered, then her children were making her come. She never had any motivation, and the little bit her children had seems to have passed. You can't chase her and insist on treating her. Let her go."

Twenty years later, I would follow that advice except that I would make one last call to "The Baby-sitter." I would say I knew Dolores did not want treatment now, but that if memory problems or behaving in ways she didn't understand came to bother her too much, I thought I could help with those. Many patients disappear because they're not ready for therapy but eventually return. With "multiples," you never know what other personalities might be listening at the moment, ready to exercise more control later. I'd make it clear she would be welcome to come back to see me any time. Then I'd "let her go."

However, as a trainee, I did exactly as I was instructed. But I had a terrible time of it. Internally, I did not let go. The pain and fear in the ER charts haunted me. I worried that Dolores might attack Dave again, or—worse yet—the little ones. More selfishly, I was sorry to have missed the chance to work with such a fascinating disorder. I believed it extremely rare and thought I'd never see another case.

This would hardly be so. As a hypnotherapist at a time of increasing awareness of multiple personality, I've treated a number of these patients. One of them, Terese, is described in Chapter 6. I was never to see Dolores Travers again, but she stayed in my mind over the years while I worked with other multiples. As I, and the profession, learned more about this disorder, I came to understand the probable origins of Dolores's condition.

Dolores's parents either rejected her or died before she was placed in the institution as a toddler. Her scars bore witness to brutal attacks, most likely by out-of-control psychotic adults, possibly by sadistic staff also. Multiple personality patients virtually all report prolonged abuse, beginning in early childhood. They have the ability to block it out with amnesia: my earlier patient Nancy had taken the first step toward this disorder. With extensive trauma, people need to create other entities to fill the increasing blank periods. There must have been good times for Dolores, too, because she developed the capacities to love and have fun. Some of the staff, adult inmates, and older children must have been kind to her. However, she had no consistency or reliable protection. This is when other personalities would have formed to handle traumas that overwhelmed Dolores. Unburdened, she could again be receptive to pleasant events.

Many multiples report that one or more of their personalities began as an imaginary companion. Dolly might have originated as a fantasized playmate who distracted Dolores from unhappiness. While most of us let our imaginary companions fade as we grow up, under the torments of the institution, Dolores might have gradually allowed herself to take on the role of Dolly, who then charmed those around her also. Multiples' other personalities are often modeled on real people. The Brain-Damaged Patient, with whom I and other hospital staff interacted, may well have begun as Dolores's imitation of one of the retarded adults at the institution who avoided harassment by uncomprehending disengagement. Often one personality fills the need for a nurturer and protector. The Baby-sitter may have served that role, first comforting Dolores and other young orphans, later mothering Dolores's children. One personality may carry the single worst trauma, such as remaining stuck in that moment at age five when a blow to the head left Dolores half deaf and in excruciating pain. Rageful personalities—like the knife-wielding Assailant—often bear abuse by vowing to retaliate when they grow bigger. Alternating handedness is a cue that different personalities are in control.

Dolores's personalities were an invaluable defense for facing the horrors of the institution. However, they followed her out into the world. There they continued to react and overreact to more ordinary stresses. Dolores probably knew she lost control of herself at times and was disturbed by memory lapses. However, most multiples are used to this by adulthood and don't tell anyone about it. Dolores's childhood had not prepared her to trust.

One characteristic Dolores shared, not only with other multiples but also with many abuse survivors, including Nancy, was a tendency to get involved with violent partners. Since the "stranger" arriving at their house used the name Dolly, it was apparently she who had gotten pregnant by age fifteen and said "yes" to at least three men who proposed marriage. She gave mean-tempered men the benefit of the doubt, most likely because she didn't remember their worst offenses. Her first two husbands were swinish by the children's account. The third, who presumably Dolly married during her eastern stay, may have been deadly. Other multiples have been known to respond to an assaultive husband by switching to an alternate personality, who leaves immediately, some without bothering to file for divorce—after all, *she* was not married to the man. If the Assailant had ever attacked anyone before, it would probably have been in legitimate self-defense and therefore unlikely to have been reported.

However, on that evening in 1978, *something* triggered the Assailant in that benign family scene. It could have been some combination of the smell of onions frying in chicken fat, the pattern in Dave's shirt, the angle at which he was sitting, a phrase one of them uttered that conjured up a terrible memory. Dolores doubtless thought Dave was someone else as she chased him. Frances may have been invisible to Dolores because she corresponded to no one in the flashback.

Dolores's children had more opportunity than anyone else to observe their mother's variability and memory lapses. Frances probably felt protective and secretive about these from the start. And she may have had bad experiences trying to explain to professionals that led her to treat us as a strange breed who had to stumble upon everything for ourselves.

Obviously, I'll never know how exactly this reconstruction describes Dolores's experience, but I think it's close. Dolores had nothing to gain by faking the discovery of deafness over and over. She had a lot to lose by pretending to forget a husband she probably already knew could be violent. Some form of epilepsy was the only other feasible diagnosis; although this could produce a short violent episode, it couldn't account for anything like the Baby-sitter.

What became of Dolores? Research suggests that once these patients make it to middle age, they have an easier time. The most turbulent stage of the disorder is usually the early twenties. When the young adults move away from their traumatic environment, they often begin to remember abuse and to become uncomfortably aware of their other personalities. Suicide attempts and substance abuse are common then. In middle age, these problems decrease even if untreated; there is often less switching. Personalities have become used to one another and may cooperate. Dolores obviously had charm, smarts, and an ability to care for herself and others that I never saw. She probably continued to be a valuable part of her lively, warm family. But I don't know this for sure, and I do often wonder.

Therapy is much like the rest of life: many people who cross our path don't stay for a neat conclusion. There are as many unfinished stories as completed ones.

3
Taking Off

Lena Winthrop wore an elegantly cut black linen suit with a single strand of pearls to her first appointment with me. Her high cheekbones, wide-set eyes, and patrician bearing reminded me of Katharine Hepburn in her middle years. Most clients are nervous in their first psychotherapy session. Lena appeared quite self-possessed.

"My husband, Henry, insisted that I see a hypnotherapist for this terrible fear of getting on an airplane. Hypnosis got him to lose thirty pounds five years ago, so he thinks it's some marvelous kind of sorcery."

"Are you interested in being able to fly?" I asked. The

suggestion that she had come to therapy under duress was a poor prognostic sign.

"Oh, definitely, I have to! My father is terminally ill with cancer. If my mother calls, I need to be able to go on a moment's notice. The sense of urgency about getting over this silly thing is mine, but it's Henry's idea to do it with hypnosis. He's a bank executive, and he's used to taking charge. He called his old hypnotherapist in New York and asked for the name of someone near Houston. His doctor recommended you, and Galveston is just an hour away. So here I am." I'd been in my first job at the University of Texas Medical School less than a year, so I was still quite flattered by personal referrals.

"Well, why don't you tell me more about yourself and about your fear of airplanes? Then we can figure out whether hypnosis would be a good thing to try first." I had detected a hint of a European accent, but I couldn't place which country or even be sure it wasn't just an affectation related to Lena's aristocratic style. I asked, "Where are you from originally?"

"New York City is where I grew up. It's where Henry and I were living until his company transferred him here six years ago to head up petroleum investments. My parents still live there. But if you mean where are *they* from, they're Russian." This fit—she indeed had the coloring called white Russian, which reminds one that the country is separated by only a narrow gulf from Scandinavia.

"Mother and Dad fled St. Petersburg when the Czar was killed. I was born seven years later. They still spoke Russian most of the time in the house. When they used English, it was with a heavy accent. So I sound Russian even though I've never been there."

"What do you remember about your childhood?"

"I was an only child. I stayed home with my parents much of the time because I was sick a lot and also I just felt different from American kids. I did go to nursery school early and then a private girls' school. They also sent me to piano, ballet, and art classes. They were big on my education—not to have a career, just to be a cultured wife for a powerful man." She laughed ironically. "I guess they succeeded."

For the next twenty minutes, Lena filled me in on the details of her childhood and her current life. Finally I returned her to the present issue: "Have you always been afraid of flying?"

"Yes, I think so. I mean, I was born in nineteen twenty-five—plane travel wasn't common when I was young." The year was 1979, so she was fifty-four, a bit older than her costly grooming had allowed me to register. "I do remember when I was dating Henry in college, he wanted us to go skiing at Christmas break once and that would have been on an airplane, so I didn't consider it."

"Have you ever flown?"

"No. The closest I came was getting on a plane once about a year after we had moved to Houston. I was going to visit my parents. I boarded immediately when they called first class, and I was okay initially. But the closer it got to takeoff, the more anxious I became. Finally, just before they were going to pull away from the gate, I was so terrified I couldn't stand it. I got out of my seat and went to the door, which they had closed. I told the stewardesses they had to bring the stairs back and let me off. I said I had a heart condition that was acting up. I don't know why I said that—it wasn't true. I just couldn't admit to the crew that I was simply panicking. They did let me off, but it delayed the departure. Then the airport physician wanted to examine me, and I knew there was nothing wrong. He asked what my 'heart condition' was, and I had to tell him I'd made it up. It was so awful and humiliating that I haven't considered getting on a plane again." The last was delivered in a tone of voice so nonchalant she could have been reciting a shopping list. She didn't look the least anxious or embarrassed, as people usually do when reliving their phobias.

"Can you tell me more about what exactly you are afraid of?" Lena hesitated, looking puzzled. To focus her answer, I gave some examples. "I mean, do you picture the plane crashing, is the cabin size claustrophobic, would you be stuck with too many people, are you afraid of heights in general?"

"None of those really. I don't think I'm claustrophobic or afraid of heights. I ride elevators with no trouble, and I'm always at some party on the balcony of a fortieth-floor penthouse. It's something more nameless, just this terrible sense of dread. Somehow it's connected to the plane going up. I hate to even watch that. If I'm near an airport and see a plane ascending rapidly, I feel so horrified for the people on it." She shuddered and crossed her arms tightly, visibly anxious for the first time. "I feel like I'd die if I flew, but I don't actually think about crashes. I don't think about anything at all—I just panic."

The most common phobias are exaggerations of fears programmed by evolution: our ancestors did have reason to be vigilant against falling off a cliff, being crushed in a collapsing cave, or being bitten by a poisonous serpent.

There is strong evidence that some people are genetically predisposed to heightened anxiety. Specific fears may even be inherited. Researchers in the Minnesota Twin Study interviewed more than a hundred pairs of identical twins separated at birth. They found that a remarkable amount of the time, when one twin has a particular phobia, the other twin fears exactly the same thing. A predisposition to panic at spiders or heights appears to be mysteriously encoded in their genes.

A second category of phobia is akin to post-traumatic stress disorder—patients have personal histories with the feared objects: they almost drowned, were locked in a dark closet repeatedly, or narrowly survived a fire or car crash. These people may have a heightened fear of that particular danger or other things randomly related to it. I have seen patients fearful of staircases and even pink-painted rooms because they had been traumatized in those settings. Other phobics are upset by patently innocuous objects with only symbolic relevance for the patient. Freud's Little Hans was terrified to go outside for fear a horse might bite him, which Freud traced as arising from his association of horses with potent masculinity.

Flying lies in a more intermediate zone of dangerousness. It is not as likely to harm you as a poisonous snake, but it's hardly risk-free. Being propelled at speeds of 600 miles an hour 20,000 feet above the earth, dependent on pressurized air for survival, might be inherently terrifying to all of us if our minds truly took in the reality. Instead, we process it more as if we were sitting in someone's living room with a noisy fan on while the TV shows pictures of tiny patchwork crop fields or clouds. The reason it doesn't register more viscerally is that we have no evolu-

tionary conditioning for it. Therefore, most airplane phobias are actually more related to one of the primal fears.
Many sufferers can tell you their aversion to planes is
caused by fear of heights, crowded spaces, or going far
from home. A minority are just uniquely afraid of airplanes. My current patient belonged in this last category.

Lena Winthrop had moved away from the image of an
ascending plane and recovered her composure. "You can
see why I must get over this thing now. In the past it never
mattered much. I'm used to the Sunset Express train to
New York. It's really rather chic. And Henry flies so much
on business—all of their other petroleum investments are
in the Middle East—that he's usually happy to vacation no
further than our beach house at Corpus Christi. But I need
to be available for my parents."

"How is your father's impending death affecting you?"
I asked. She hadn't yet addressed this emotion-laden
topic.

"Oh, I've pretty well accepted it," she replied calmly,
discouraging further inquiry. "He's eighty-three, the chemotherapy has stopped working, and the tumors have spread
all through his body. It's his time. It could happen any-
where in the next few weeks to months at most. I just don't
want to let either of them down with this foolishness, so we
need to change it fast. I'll be happy to pay double your
usual fee."

"That won't be necessary." I tried to mask my annoy-
ance at her implication that she could buy better treatment
than others would receive. The alternate interpretation of
her offer was that Lena simply felt it fair that she pay according to her means, but she didn't seem like much of a
socialist. I decided not to get into it. "There are a number

of approaches we could use in treating a phobia; maybe I should take some time to explain the others to you."

"No. Henry's doctor sent me here for hypnosis. I want to try that, unless you're sure that it wouldn't work on me." Lena presented the paradoxical mix I've noted in many aristocratic women, behaving in a commanding manner while using language about acquiescence to others. Still, her request was quite reasonable.

"Okay, we can certainly start with that next session to see how hypnotizable you are. I just want you to know it's not the only effective treatment. If you turn out not to be very hypnotizable, there are several other things that will probably help."

Since she had stressed how much time mattered, I gave Lena an appointment later that week. After she walked out, I turned to watch her through the window facing the parking lot. A person's gait and gestures in unguarded moments often reveal much about his or her character. It can be as subtle as a slump of the shoulders once one is alone or as dramatic as kicking at parked cars after exiting a session. This time, I observed only that Lena's regal bearing held up at a distance. More interesting, I saw her approach a Cadillac with tinted windows. A uniformed chauffeur jumped out to open the door for Lena and guided her into the backseat. As the big car glided away, I wondered if this were an extravagance she thought necessary to her social station or whether she might be phobic of driving also. Occasionally, fears of planes extend to other vehicles. I made a note to ask her next time.

The most common treatment for flying phobia is antianxiety medication. Valium and its descendants often

work on fears of objects or situations that need to be confronted only rarely, so the patient doesn't take the medication long enough to risk addiction. For ongoing
phobias, pharmacologic treatment usually involves one of
the serotonin reuptake inhibiting antidepressants, of
which Prozac is the best known. These affect anxiety as
well as depression. These are less addictive, if less dramatic in effect, than Valium. As a psychologist, I could not
prescribe medication but could refer patients to my psychiatrist colleagues at the Medical School. However, several kinds of psychotherapy are as effective as drug
treatment without the possible side effects.

One, systematic desensitization, begins with teaching
people conscious control of relaxation processes—such as
decreasing muscle tension and slowing and deepening
breathing. Then patients construct a hierarchy of threatening situations—for instance, from looking out a second-
floor window to being near the edge of a sixtieth-floor
balcony—and practice confronting each level in turn
while utilizing their physical relaxation skills. Another type
of therapy, cognitive-behavioral, teaches a patient to recognize reflexive, unrealistic thoughts that generate anxiety
("Everybody else at this party will be completely at ease,
and if they notice I'm nervous, they'll despise me") and to
substitute more realistic ones ("Other people will be feeling shy, too. Admitting I'm shy may elicit friendliness from
others").

Hypnosis is not used as often as these other two approaches to treat phobias, largely because fewer therapists
are trained in hypnotherapy; however, it can be equally
helpful. Dr. Fred Frankel of Harvard has done research
finding that phobics are more hypnotizable on the aver-

age than other people. He speculates that these people's superior ability to visualize disasters occurring actually helps them maintain their fears. Hypnotherapy has the power to harness this ability in the service of calming imagery. There was a good chance hypnosis would work with Lena Winthrop. However, if not, we would switch to a cognitive-behavioral or systematic desensitization approach.

Lena arrived promptly for her second session. "Well, I'm ready to start. What do we do?"

I explained that we would begin with an induction to see how hypnotizable she was. If she went into a trance fairly quickly, we would spend most of the time exploring why she was afraid of flying. In subsequent sessions, I would begin to suggest that the fear would diminish. "Before we get started," I added, "I have one question. I noticed your chauffeur last time; are you nervous about driving?"

"Oh, no, I'd prefer to drive myself, but Henry doesn't think it looks proper. He's afraid people will think we can't afford a driver."

"And he decides whether you drive?"

"Well, he'd never insist if my heart was set on something. But he's so accommodating about taking trains and cars everywhere. He's been rearranging his schedule for the last year around my dad's illness. I feel like I should do what he wants on these kinds of things. Our social life is so intertwined with his business."

My office contained a velvet-upholstered antique armchair, in which Lena was already seated, and an "analyst's" couch much like the one Freud used for his free association process—but also well suited to hypnosis. "You can stay in the chair or lie on that couch, whichever looks the most comfortable to you," I told her.

"This chair is just fine," she said. It was high-backed enough that one could not fall once relaxed, but the couch was easily the more *physically* comfortable spot. About half my clients chose the chair as the more *psychologically* comfortable. I had already pegged Lena as a chair type.

"You see that pin on the wall directly in front of you?" Two little gold pushpins were permanently positioned— one in front of the chair and the other in the ceiling over the couch. "I want you to stare at the pin as you begin to relax." I continued in a gentle monotone. "Let the muscles of your feet and toes relax. . . . Let the relaxation spread up through your ankles and calves. . . . Let all the muscles of your knees relax. . . . Let your thighs and hips relax so that all of the tension flows out of your legs and they are completely limp and loose and comfortable." I slowly talked her through relaxing each of her body parts, alternating this with suggestions that her breathing become slower and deeper.

"Finally, the muscles of your eyelids are beginning to relax also, as if a weight were pulling them gently down, getting heavier and heavier." Lena blinked slowly, and her eyes reopened only halfway. "They will get heavier and heavier until they close completely." They fluttered and shut—much more quickly than with the average hypnotizee. I talked her through the same staircase imagery for deepening the trance that I had used with Nancy.

"Now I want you to begin to focus on that feeling of

fear associated with flying. Picture watching a plane ascend and thinking what you'd feel like on it." I was ready to pull her back from this imagery at any moment if it was too frightening. She looked anxious but not terrified, so I proceeded. "Now stay with that fearful feeling and let it form a bridge to take you back to some other place and time when you felt the same way. Just travel back on the fear until you find a scene that will tell us something about why you don't want to be on an airplane. Then take time to notice where you are, see your surroundings, watch what's going on there. You'll be able to describe it in a slow, clear voice without disturbing the hypnosis. Now, just tell me, where are you?"

"I'm in the cockpit of the plane." I bolted to attention as she continued. "I'm just strapping myself into the pilot's seat."

I had no idea what to make of this. People usually go to actual memories with these instructions, but I wondered if Lena was an exception. In the absence of another idea, I proceeded with the next standard question. "Is anyone there with you?"

"The instructor, Mr. Dalton, is sitting to my left."

"What is he doing?"

"Nothing, he's just watching me. He's not supposed to give me any directions unless I start to make a mistake."

"And what are you doing?"

"I'm cranking the left engine. It catches, and the tach settles down at eight hundred rpm. Right engine next. It catches and settles at eight hundred. The tanks are full. I set the altimeter."

"Lena, how old are you in this scene you're in?"

"I'm a senior in high school. I'm seventeen."

This struck me as unlikely, but everything else I was hearing sounded like a memory. I decided to sort out the veracity later and stay with the inquiry. I was sure to learn something about her phobia. "What happens next?"

"I release the brakes and taxi slowly toward the runway. I run up the throttle on the left engine and check rpm and manifold pressure. Then the right engine—same thing.

"I look at Mr. Dalton. He smiles encouragingly. I'm cleared for takeoff. We're rolling—I reach ninety knots. I ease back on the controls, and the plane lifts off the ground! God, it's really different from the flight simulator!

"We're climbing. At five hundred feet I recheck my instruments. I can see everything beneath us. The airfield's back to the left. The cemetery's in front of it. Way ahead of me are the Long Island Sound and the bridge." Her voice had become excited and more spontaneous. Her usual measured tone was gone.

"What do you do now?"

"I hold my climb steady at a hundred knots. I'm supposed to level off at fifteen hundred feet. I look at the altimeter. Oh, my God, we're passing a thousand feet! I feel a pain in my chest. I'm clutching my chest, yelling at Mr. Dalton that I'm going to have a heart attack." Lena was not actually clutching her chest. She had not been enacting any of this overtly, as someone more completely age-regressed might do. She sat immobile in the chair as she narrated. "Mr. Dalton doesn't understand me over the noise of the engines, but he knows something's wrong. He's signaling me to bring the plane down, but I can't. I think I'm going to die!" At this point she appeared terrifyingly caught up in the imagery.

"You can stay aware of this scene while also aware of yourself here with me," I told her. "You can remember you're a fifty-four-year-old adult now, who is safe. You are just watching yourself in this other time and place. What happens next?"

"I'm not sure what happened." She sounded calmer. "I'm on the ground now. I guess Mr. Dalton took over and landed the plane. He's asking me what's wrong. I say that I was going to have a heart attack and die. He tells me that I just panicked. He says we'll stop for today and try the flight again. I tell him no, I'm never going up again—I could have died. Except I know that's not exactly true. I just felt that way."

"Okay, now I want you to begin to leave that scene in the airplane; let it fade from your mind's eye for now. But when you wake up, you will be able to remember it clearly in as much detail as you want." I talked her through more relaxation and then counted her awake.

She blinked and readjusted herself to an upright position in the chair. "My, that was something! It was like I was really back there."

"Back where?"

"In my patriots' flying class."

"You really flew a plane?"

"Barely—I dropped out after that day. But I'd done all the paper-and-pencil course work and the flight simulator runs. If I'd just done the six practice flights, I'd have qualified." She sounded wistful.

"Qualified for what exactly?"

"To be a domestic pilot and free up all the male pilots for the air force. It was World War II."

"They let seventeen-year-old girls fly back then?"

"Eighteen. When I graduated high school and turned eighteen, I would have done forty more hours of supervised flying and been a pilot. They came into the schools telling us about all these 'patriots' class' things for girls to do stateside. I sure didn't want to go work in a factory assembly line, but flying all over the country sounded like the most exciting thing I'd ever heard of."

"Your parents approved?"

"Well, no, they didn't like the idea. They signed the permission form for the class, but they hadn't really agreed that I'd go to work as a pilot. They said maybe just summers. They still thought that I should go straight to college. But all the guys my age were going off to the army. They'd be coming back to college in a couple years. I figured I might as well go when they did. Flying seemed like a lot more fun. And more important, too. I felt very patriotic, wanting to do something for the war effort. My parents didn't think that way. They were alienated from both the U.S. and communist Russia, so they didn't see it as our duty to defend either. But I felt like it would finally make me a genuine American. God, it was terrible to give up. I don't think I've ever wanted to do anything as much in my whole life."

"Had you forgotten?"

"Goodness, no! I always remembered."

"You didn't tell me about it when I asked why you were afraid of planes or asked whether you'd ever flown."

"This is going to sound crazy, but I never made the connection. I thought *that* was being afraid of being a pilot, *this* was being afraid of being a passenger. I realize now it's the same fear—of the plane going up. It doesn't matter if I'm the one flying. Something about watching that altimeter pass one thousand feet just panicked me."

One of the early psychoanalysts, Harry Stack Sullivan, wrote about a concept he called selective inattention. He acknowledged that people can completely repress disturbing experiences, as Freud had described. However, Sullivan believed that much more often they behave in a similar manner with events they fully remember—ignoring them or avoiding thinking through their implications to retain their peace of mind. Sullivan describes a patient who began each session by confessing that he had just seen a male stranger on a train whom he fantasized about kissing, then biting. The patient was amazed anew each week that such a thought could enter his head although, when reminded, he would agree that it was virtually identical to fantasies he had experienced regularly for years. Lena certainly seemed to have exercised selective inattention to her early piloting experience.

Our hour was nearly up. "That helped us locate the beginning of your fear of planes," I told her, "but we still don't understand why you got frightened the first time. Next session we'll spend more time exploring that before we get to direct suggestions for eliminating the phobia. I'm going to a long weekend conference in Atlanta, so I won't be here at the start of the week. How about meeting on Wednesday? I could do it at either one or three o'clock."

"Three would be perfect. Since you're going away, maybe I should pay my bill today so you'll have some spending money for shopping there."

"That won't be necessary. The medical school will be

billing you monthly." Lena was setting a pattern. This was the second time she had ended a session with an allusion to payment—overtly generous but covertly insulting. I was new enough to have some defensive desire to explain that my salary at the medical school was not tied directly to payments by patients and that I had plenty of "spending money." But I was also becoming accustomed to the fact that while other patients often elevated therapists in an idealized manner, many wealthy Texans viewed us as just another branch of their servant class. Lena's maid might have genuinely appreciated the same statement on the eve of her day off.

"I hope you have a lovely time on your trip," she said as she exited. This parting emphasis on my travel made me wonder if I had stirred up competitive feelings with my itinerary for the week. She could have correctly deduced that I would be *flying* to Atlanta.

During the busy hypnosis conference, the discussions of age regression and memory reminded me of my youthful pilot. Although Lena's plane incident seemed to be authentic, it had raised questions in my mind of how to judge the accuracy of such recall. That thorny issue is now hotly debated at hypnosis gatherings—the only topic I've ever seen provoke these normally poised professionals into yelling insults at each other. However, in 1979 it was brushed off as an unnecessary question—you were either doing "age regression" and eliciting memories or doing "hypno-projectives"—asking for an image that would explain a symptom and getting fanciful metaphors—no possible confusion.

The responses were more interesting when I asked the older women in attendance about World War II. Several remembered flying lessons being offered, although none had considered taking them. Many had pursued other career opportunities that were suddenly open to them. Some had become physicians and therapists without having considered it possible a few years earlier. They remembered a time of great vocational freedom. They also remembered the female workers being summarily dumped out of jobs when the men returned. Women who completed the medical, graduate, or dental degrees they had been encouraged to start did so over strong pressure to drop out now that they "wouldn't be needed." Wartime changes may have sown the seeds of women's liberation, but they had hardly flowered then. I understood more about Lena's era by the time she strode into my office for her next session.

"I thought a lot about your question concerning the chauffeur," she announced. This was interesting—I hadn't given a thought to the comment since I made it, despite all my musings about her. "It's kind of ironic that I set out to be a pilot and now I'm not even driving my own car. And I'm not afraid of cars. The time to trade the Cadillac in on a new model is coming up soon." Really? It looked like a brand-new car to me. "So maybe this time I'll suggest we get a little Porsche for me to drive instead." Last week she had presented the chauffeur as not a problem but rather a point of graceful acquiescence, so I stayed with her original complaint.

"Well, if you want to change that, I'm glad you've found a way. Let's see what we can do about the flying.

Have you thought any more about planes, noticed any difference, like being more or less afraid of them?"

"I might be more afraid, actually. When I think of getting a call from my parents, I really panic—maybe because I do picture getting on a plane now or maybe because last week I experienced again how awful it was the one time I flew."

"Today we can explore more about why that was. If there's enough time, I will also give you some suggestions about feeling safer, although we'll need other sessions to complete that. Let's get started. Do you still prefer the chair?"

Lena nodded and settled her body deeper into it. I talked her through the same induction as before. She appeared very relaxed. Her breathing was slow and deep.

"Now begin to picture yourself up in that plane with Mr. Dalton. You can see the airfield back to your left and the Long Island Sound way out in front of you," I told her, relying on my notes for her own words as I guided her back into the memory. "You're supposed to level off at fifteen hundred feet. You look at the gauge—it's passing one thousand feet, and you begin to feel frightened." Lena's facial muscles tightened markedly, and her hands gripped the armrests. "Now stay with that fear as you let the scene of the flying class fade from your mind's eye. Let that fear form a bridge to take you even further back, to another place and time when you felt that same way. Just move back on that fear until you stop at another scene that will tell us more about why you're afraid. Let the new scene begin to form around you. Notice your surroundings, see who's there with you. Now tell me where you are."

"I'm in my room on the bed." Her voice had a childlike quality, although it was not as uncannily like a real child speaking as Nancy's age regression had sounded.

"How old are you?"

"I'm seven. I'm in second grade, except they don't let me go to school anymore."

"Is anyone there with you?"

"Yes, Dr. Tucker's there. He's examining me. Mother's standing just inside the door watching."

"What is the doctor doing?"

"He lifts my pajama top and holds that cold, round thing against me. He puts it on my back and tells me to hold still while he listens. Then he puts it on my tummy and my chest. I don't like Dr. Tucker. He acts like my friend but every time he comes, he whispers with Mom outside and then I have to stay in bed some more. But this time he says, 'Very good, you're all well, young lady. It's time you were up and around.' "

"Well from what?"

"Umatic fever." Lena had told me in the first session that she was often ill in her childhood but hadn't mentioned rheumatic fever specifically.

"Dr. Tucker says, 'Can I talk to you, Mrs. Romanov?' He and Mom step out into the hall like always. She pulls the door shut—almost. I sit up on the foot of the bed closer to the door so I can hear. I'm afraid he lied and is going to tell her to make me stay in bed some more."

"Do you hear what he does say?"

"Yeah, he says, 'There's no sign of a murmur.' " Her voice has taken on a mockingly pompous tone. " 'I think you could send her to school, half a day at first so she doesn't get tired. But remember: her heart is always going to be weak. I'll write a letter to the school telling them she needs to be permanently excused from any sports. And you mustn't let her play boisterous games with other children.' He says, 'She must never get on an airplane—the altitude, the thin oxygen—it could kill her with that heart.' " Back in her childish voice, she continued. "That sends a shudder through me! I picture dying."

"What happens next?"

"I don't know. It sort of stops there." Her voice sounded more adult now.

"Okay, you can let the scene completely fade from your mind for now. Later you will be able to remember it clearly, but you will know that it was long, long ago. Planes weren't pressurized then, but now they are. You can feel confident that what Dr. Tucker said then isn't meant for today. I want you to leave his warning far, far behind you. Now I'm going to ask you to wake up as I count backwards from ten to one." I slowly counted her awake. Her eyes popped open in a look of amazement.

"I hadn't thought about that since I was a little girl. I think I worried about dying for weeks after that. Gradually, though, I just didn't think about it anymore—except that day in the plane, it came back to me. I suddenly remembered Dr. Tucker had said I'd die if I flew. I never thought about it to realize that's why I'm afraid."

"You did have rheumatic fever?"

"Yes, I was out of school for three months."

"Well, planes' cabins weren't pressurized then. Maybe it would have been dangerous for you in the early ones."

"Oh, no!" She corrected me quite forcefully. "That awful man didn't know what he was talking about even for back then. He was probably just scared of flying himself. When planes weren't pressurized, passenger aircraft didn't fly at today's altitudes. The DC-3s rarely went over five thousand feet; there's no problem with oxygen until ten thousand." I thought I had heard of prohibitions against heart patients flying as standard advice in the past. However, Lena seemed quite certain, and there was no point in debating previous risks when I was trying to focus on present safety.

"Has your current physician told you it's all right to fly?"

"Of course. See—I don't have heart damage. That's another reason I say Dr. Tucker didn't know what he was talking about. God, I hadn't thought about those clammy, damp hands and that cold stethoscope in years. He was my pediatrician then. I think he just said that to anyone who'd had rheumatic fever. Dad always worried whether I was getting good care 'cause Dr. Tucker didn't work out of the classy clinic." I could see where Lena got some of her attitudes. "A year later, Dad paid a lot to take me to a cardiologist for an examination, and he said my heart was fit as a horse's. Two-thirds of patients do get permanent damage from it. I was one of the lucky ones. That gym excuse thing and don't play *boisterously* went by the wayside then."

"But you told the stewardesses you had a 'heart condition.' "

A look of recognition passed over her face. "Oh, God, that's why I said that!"

"But did you feel like you were having a heart attack that time?"

"No, the thought that I could went through my mind for a moment, but then I thought I'd made it up. In my practice flight, I really felt like my heart was clutching up.

I remembered what Dr. Tucker had said, and I didn't have time to remind myself it wasn't true—I just panicked."

"But you didn't think he might be right? That had nothing to do with your dropping out?"

"No, once I was on the ground I didn't even know why I'd panicked. I just didn't want to get that scared again and feel like such a failure. My heart wasn't one of Mother and Dad's considerations when deciding whether to sign the consent form. Like I said, they'd known I was okay after we saw the cardiologist in third grade. By high school, I was on the girls' basketball team. Of course, maybe what he said, or the rheumatic fever at least, had something to do with why Mother was always so anxious and overprotective of me."

"Well, now we can begin to reverse that sense of your needing to be protected from things like flying. Next time we'll give you lots more suggestions about leaving the fear behind, and I'll talk you through a hypnotic version of a comfortable, safe airplane flight. Then we'll make you a self-hypnosis tape to use on an actual airplane."

"I don't think that's necessary. I really don't feel afraid anymore now that I realize where I got that foolish idea. I could fly today."

"It's great you feel that way, but it's important to reinforce it so the fear stays gone. If you want to keep to the frequent schedule, we could meet Monday at this time."

"Okay. I'm happy to see you again. Of course, you deserve to hear how everything goes. But I really think I'm over the flying fear. And now I know why I've always hated doctors, too."

"It strikes me that the components of that memory are all intertwined in the current situation," I ventured. "Not just the airplanes, but you will be headed toward illness, doctors, and someone who's dying."

"Yes, when I think what it must be like for Dad, I do associate it with my childhood illnesses. But it doesn't frighten me anymore. I feel strong enough to deal with these things." Her voice broke slightly. "Now Dad's the helpless one." She pulled a monogrammed handkerchief out of her purse and dabbed away a lone tear with her usual dignified composure as she arose. "Well, I will see you Monday."

It was the first session she had left without some covertly condescending allusion to money. I watched through the window as the chauffeur jumped out of the Cadillac and scurried to open the door when Lena approached briskly. He seemed even more superfluous than before.

Lena walked into her fourth session full of energetic plans. "I've set up a practice flight," she announced. I was startled by her use of the same phrase with which she had described her pilot lessons. However, she meant something more mundane this time. "I'm going to visit my friend Marge who lives in San Antonio next week while Henry is away on business. I've always driven to San Antonio, but it's only a thirty-minute flight."

I had talked to her about taking a short flight first, but after more preparation by hypnotic imagery. "Are you sure you're ready for that?"

"Oh yes! It will make a good start, and then, within a couple weeks, I want to go up to New York. Dad's actually doing a little better. They've changed the chemotherapy, and the new combination has made the tumors regress again. No one is suggesting that he will survive the cancer, but now it looks like he has more time, and he's certainly more comfortable. I'd like to visit them while he's enjoying this remission. I've also been thinking about joining Henry on one of his business trips. He's always wanted me to, and he goes to such interesting places. I think it would be thrilling to put on a veil and see the Arab world."

Lena's enthusiasm was so contagious that I questioned whether it was necessary to complete my original treatment plan. With most phobias, the discovery stage is just a beginning. It takes time to decondition the fear gradually with repeated positive experiences in hypnotic imagery. For example, I once met daily for a week with a San Francisco attorney who had become stranded in Houston after her mild plane phobia had escalated to a total inability to board a plane and then further into blind panic at the idea of any form of transportation when she had tried to rent a car to drive back. It took one session to explore childhood memories about her sister dying during the night in the bedroom they shared after symptoms similar to the stomach cramps that now accompanied the attorney's panic attacks. Another session had illuminated what present stressors in her relationships at work and with her boyfriend led to her feeling inadequately cared for and exposed to risk. We had then spent the remaining five sessions going through imagery of getting into a taxi, riding to the airport, and boarding a plane while remaining calm and aware that her own stomachache was innocuous. Between sessions, she practiced hailing a cab, making a dry run through the airport, and booking her flight. After successfully flying home, she spent the next six months resolving issues about her sister's death with a San Francisco therapist.

In Lena's case, simply reliving the memories and realizing their connection to her phobia was so cathartic that it seemed to have released her from the fear. However, I certainly wanted to do a brief version of deconditioning imagery before her "practice flight." Since this was therapy and not research, the goal was to make totally sure she was prepared to fly. There was no reason to test whether her unusually strong response to memory and insight might be sufficient. I told Lena that I would tape the hypnosis we did in this session for her to listen to both before flying and once she was actually on the plane.

I first asked her for details about the flight that I would build into my imagery, such as what size the plane was and what she would be taking along with her to read. As she relaxed into the chair which was still her choice of furniture (some patients do switch to the couch as they become less self-conscious), I repeated the usual eye-closure induction and talked her through deep relaxation procedures.

Then I suggested, "You can picture yourself arriving at the airport feeling quite relaxed and confident. You check your luggage and walk through security's metal detector thinking about how happy you are to finally be flying. When you sit down in the waiting area with your *New Yorker,* before you begin to read it, you can first note its date. That will remind you that you're flying in 1979, in a modern climate-controlled plane. You can count how many decades have passed since that misguided advice, and you can leave it in the past. When they call your flight for boarding, you can see yourself walking through the gate toward the plane. Where the walkway is attached to the door of the plane, you can see the strong, thick structure of the plane cabin. You head toward your seat noting the new, modern look of the large interior of the plane."

My aeronautic descriptions sounded comically low-tech after Lena's sophisticated terminology. However, I felt it important to intersperse specific reassurances about the date and plane construction—counteracting Lena's unique fears—with the more standard imagery of a pleasant flight, which I would describe in any plane phobia desensitization.

"Once you are settled in the roomy seat"—she had told me she was flying first class—"you can look out at the runway through the windows with their double glass two inches apart, reminding you again of the pressurized cabin. You feel calm. Your muscles are relaxed, you remember to do your slow, deep abdominal breathing. At some point, you'll hear the hiss of air begin from the little, round plastic nozzles above you; it again emphasizes the safe, climate-controlled environment. As the engines fire up, you'll hear that they're large jet ones. You can sit back, feeling very healthy, and silently say to Dr. Tucker, 'You don't know what you're talking about!' " Lena smiled gently, and a subdued chuckle emerged through the deep relaxation. As I had suspected, enlisting her hostility seemed to bolster her confidence.

"You see him fade away, leaving all that outmoded thinking far behind as the plane takes off. You feel the exhilaration of knowing you are safe and flying. Now your thoughts can turn to all the things you're going to do once you get there." I used very general wording about imagining her destination. In this session it would evoke San Antonio and visiting with Marge; however, it should also be applicable to the return flight and to future plane travel. Finally I told her, "In a minute, I'm going to ask you to wake up by counting from ten to one backwards. By the count of one, you will be wide awake but still feeling pleasantly relaxed and carrying all these good feelings about flying deep within you."

Lena opened her eyes and smiled. "That was great. Hypnosis feels so lovely, and I just made that idiot doctor vanish completely." She seemed to want to emphasize that this was now *fun* rather than in any way *necessary*. She might have been right; I saw no reason to disagree so long as she was going to listen to the recording.

"You should play this tape daily for the three days before your flight and then again once you're actually on the plane." I checked with her. "Besides the Dr. Tucker part, did the rest of the imagery work for you?"

"Yes, it really got me looking forward to the trip. Marge lives near the river walk, and we'll see all the street artists and go in the galleries. Maybe I'll find a painting Henry would like." She interrupted herself abruptly. "Did I tell you I'm getting a car? Probably a Porsche, but definitely something sporty. I learned to drive on a stick shift, so that's what I want. I'm going to look at several models next week. The chauffeur will drive me around to car lots—his last assignment!"

"How does Henry feel about all this?"

"At first he said his usual things about what will people think, but I told him if it just needed to look like we were spending a lot of money, he could get me a Ferrari instead of a Porsche. Even he could see the humor in that. And another VP's wife drives her own sports car—hers is even a convertible. It's not so outrageous. I think he's just relieved I haven't suggested learning to fly the company plane." She laughed mischievously.

"Before you go that far, I think the plan for San Antonio is a good one. Remember to listen to the tape—going and returning."

"Oh, I will. It's wonderfully pleasant, but I know I could already do it right now."

"You probably could, but, as you say, it will make it more pleasant. Will you call me as soon as you get back to Houston? I want to hear how the trip went. And you can let me know if there's anything you'd want to modify about the tape or whether it's fine for future flights. Then we'll decide if we need another appointment."

"Okay, I'll call the minute I get back and tell you all about it. And you'll get to hear what kind of car I pick out," Lena told me as she exited. I was swept up by her newfound energy, but a bit worried. I certainly thought the trip would be a success or I would have discouraged it. Still, there was always a risk that she would push herself too fast and panic.

But she didn't. "It was great!" Lena told me when she called. "Marge and I had a wonderful visit, wandering around the art studios. I listened to the tape on the plane, and the flight went perfectly. I wasn't anxious—except maybe a bit, but that's part of being excited, isn't it?"

"That's true. But it's a truth which people with phobias

aren't able to appreciate. That's a sign you've really made a change."

"Oh, I'm making lots of changes. The day before my trip, I drove two Porsches and several other cars. I think I'm going to get a little silver Porsche with white leather seats. Henry is going back with me tomorrow, when I make the final decision. I have reservations to New York a week from Thursday. I've also been talking seriously with Henry about going to the Middle East with him on one of his trips. It sounds like it would be best to visit Egypt first. You can wear your usual clothes, they're very used to tourists, and I've always been fascinated with the pyramids. Then I might work my way up to the really different cultures, like Saudi Arabia.

"I've also decided that eventually I'm going to Russia. I've always wanted to, but I couldn't with the flying problem. And I thought my parents would see it as a betrayal to go there while the communists are in control, even though I'm not very political myself. Actually, it's mostly Dad who is so bitter about what they took away. I wouldn't want to go that far away while he's sick. But after he's gone, Mother might understand. She might even be glad to have me look up distant relatives or to get to see pictures of their old street. And I'll have the hypnosis tape for Aeroflot."

"Do you want to meet again for anything, or are you all set?"

"I've felt all set since the third session. I'll let you know how the other trips go. Thanks so much." She rang off.

Released from her flying phobia, Lena was reclaiming the adventurous spirit of her earlier self. That one failure in pilot training had tilted her toward accepting the more limited expectations first of her parents and later of Henry. Once she realized how unnecessary that initial sacrifice of freedom had been, her natural boldness blossomed. I got a postcard from a trip to the Middle East months later. I never got one from Russia—maybe the KGB intercepted it.

4

Mourning Sickness

"I think I may be pregnant," announced George when he called the Texas Medical School's Department of Obstetrics and Gynecology. "Or maybe it's a false pregnancy; I just want a doctor to examine me and say for sure." The disconcerted obstetrician referred him to the hospital's Gender Disorders Center. This name was largely a euphemism for the sex-change operations that made up the majority of the Center's business; however, they were expected to handle a variety of sexual eccentricities. George was scheduled for a day of diagnostic tests, medical exams, and psychological evaluations. A few minutes into the first interview, the Center's psychologist, Don Greer, called me. "We have a man here with pseudocyesis who says it started when a doctor hypnotized him." I finished my morning's duties on the psychiatric inpatient unit and hurried over to join the evaluation in progress.

The medical diagnosis of "pseudocyesis" (from the Latin *pseudo* = false and *cyesis* = pregnancy) requires both a false belief that one is pregnant and the presence of some physical changes characteristic of pregnancy. Common symptoms in women are disappearance of monthly menstrual periods; gradual abdominal swelling; breast changes such as enlargement, tenderness, secretion of small amounts of milk, or darkening of the nipples; a sensation of fetal movement; morning nausea and vomiting; increase in appetite; and weight gain. Hypnotherapy has often been a successful treatment for false pregnancy, but it had never before been reported as a cause. Not surprisingly, most victims of false pregnancy are female.

The most common male equivalent is a psychosomatic illness called "couvade syndrome," in which the husband of an expectant woman experiences some of these physical symptoms—abdominal swelling and discomfort, unusual food cravings, morning nausea, and occasionally breast enlargement. He may experience violent stomach cramps during the time his wife is in labor. However, the couvade victim does not think he is pregnant and usually doesn't even notice the analogy to his wife's pregnancy until it is called to his attention.

Men can also have beliefs about being pregnant without any accompanying physical symptoms. This can occur in schizophrenia or other psychotic disorders. For example, a recent patient on our psychiatric inpatient ward had claimed to be pregnant by Elvis Presley. The King was still alive at the time, but it's not clear this would have been necessary from the patient's point of view. He was an exuberant little man who joyously greeted everyone walking onto the locked unit with this news. The pregnancy was just one of his delusional beliefs, and he was diagnosed as being in the manic phase of manic-depressive illness, not as having pseudocyesis.

Full-blown (so to speak) male false pregnancy is extremely rare. By 1979, when George appeared at our center, only three cases had been reported in medical articles. These men showed all the physical symptoms that women with false pregnancy do—with the obvious exception of menstrual cessation. We appeared to have a fourth case in our examining room.

George was six feet, two inches tall, a bony but muscular man of about forty. Decades in the Texas sun had bleached what must have been red hair to a strange mound of light orange-blond straw. His craggy face barely showed its original freckles under a mass of overlapping brown, leathery blotches burned on in defiance of his complexion's resistance to tanning. He wore jeans and a loose work shirt and, despite his rugged features, looked distinctly . . . well, pregnant, like a real-life version of those movies where Arnold Schwarzenegger or Burt Reynolds dresses up with a pillow under his clothing. Not only did George not have a pillow under his shirt but the physician who had done a physical examination told me, "He looks a lot more pregnant with his clothes off."

A medical resident told me the same thing. *And* several wide-eyed students described George's physical exam. At a teaching hospital, the rarity of the disorder predicts how many doctors and doctors-to-be will see a patient. An assortment of staff in various specialties had examined, reexamined, and observed the reexamination of George. Many ingenious minds determined the relevant battery of laboratory tests for male pseudocyesis. George appeared embarrassed but good-natured about all the attention: "It's good they're being really thorough. That way, I'll know for sure by the end of the day if I'm pregnant or not."

George's physical exam was normal except for his enlarged abdomen and some breast development, with one breast larger than the other. All laboratory tests, including measurements of male and female sex hormones, were normal for a man. The visual image he presented was not entirely consistent with any one stage of pregnancy. George had experienced his symptoms for three months; yet his abdomen was as swollen as that of a woman six months pregnant; his breast enlargement was like that of a budding eleven- or thirteen-year-old girl (depending on which side you looked at); and his backward-leaning, waddling gait was that of a woman about to deliver any day.

"I went to this hypnotist, Dr. Branden, to quit smoking, and that's how the pregnancy began," George told me. The hypnotic session had occurred three months before our evaluation. "He told me to close my eyes and talked about waves of relaxation going through me. I really felt like I was made of water. Then he told me I'd find cigarettes disgusting. If I even tried to smoke one, my lungs would react by rejecting the smoke. He talked about how I'd feel healthy and my lungs would start to cleanse themselves. I could see this picture of spongy black lungs changing to fresh pink."

Toward the end of the session, Dr. Branden told

George to imagine "the person you would like to be." The image of a pregnant woman popped into his mind. George remembered hypnotic suggestions that he could "become this person," but at no point had Dr. Branden asked his patient to describe this ideal.

"A few hours after I left the doctor's office, I noticed my stomach seemed big. It got bigger and bigger over the next three months." George also developed morning nausea, a watery secretion from his nipples, and a "throbbing like a heartbeat" in his abdomen. And, yes, he had quit smoking.

"Now every day when I want to unwind, I close my eyes, relax as much as I can—kind of like the hypnosis—and picture myself as if I'm looking in a mirror and I'm a pregnant woman." This description resembled the directions for practicing self-hypnosis that patients are sometimes urged to do to reinforce the hypnotist's suggestions. However, George did not recall any instruction from Dr. Branden to practice at home. Perhaps he was told to imagine himself becoming the person he "wanted to be"—a common posthypnotic suggestion—and had forgotten that he had been told this. Or maybe he had stumbled on this practice accidentally. In any case, George did seem to be repeating the suggestion in a self-hypnotic state.

Despite using the phrase "false pregnancy" and repeatedly stating that he knew his symptoms were "not real," George wondered whether a true pregnancy might in fact be possible. "I read in the *National Enquirer* that a man was pregnant in France, and another time I read about an experiment where fertilized eggs were surgically put into male rats and they grew." George had been taking prenatal vitamins, abstaining from drinking alcohol, and following other standard advice for pregnant women. "If I really am pregnant, I guess I'd need a C-section when it's time for the baby to come, right?" His logic was flawless once you accepted his fantastic premise.

George was clearly of at least average intelligence, although his formal education had ended with the eighth grade. He worked on oil field construction sites. When drilling equipment struck oil, his crew rushed out to cap the black geyser, which initially spewed under its own compressed forces. They channeled it into massive pipe sections, eight feet in diameter. Then the crew erected— with huge steel beams—the derrick that would pump the oil once the natural pressure subsided. George's task was electrician's assistant. He climbed the half-finished derricks, hauling wire to activate the pumps. Although he was athletic and tough by most standards, in the Texas oil fields, he told me, "You wouldn't believe the guys who actually build the derricks. They look like Goliath. I'm a shrimp to them. The one who's quick with my hands and sharp."

George had the good judgment to wear loose clothes and refrain from discussing his "pregnancy" at construction sites. Nevertheless, two of his brawny co-workers had told him he was getting fat, and one had even joked that "your stomach looks as big as my wife's when she was pregnant; maybe we should loan you some maternity clothes."

George laughed off this suggestion. "But actually, even though I was kinda nervous that he had come that close to noticing what was happening, I liked the idea that someone else said I might be pregnant, even as a joke. I'd been thinking about maternity clothes—I almost wished he'd meant it about giving me some." However, George had not let his pseudocyesis interfere at work, where he was respected but a loner. He talked with candor and seemed completely sane except for his suspicion that he might actually be pregnant.

The Gender Disorders Center was housed in an aging, one-story, wooden building behind the modern hospital in which I'd conducted my sessions with Lena a few months earlier. It had been used for supply storage until the Center was tentatively founded nine years before. Its waiting room was furnished with a collection of mismatched chairs, one of them a rocker. A battered Mr. Coffee machine wafted its pungent aroma across the room, and speakers played an "oldies" rock station rather than the constant physician pages broadcast through the rest of the medical school. To most visitors, the small-town hospital seemed provincial and the Center behind it downright homey. But George had driven from the east Texas flatlands just inland from the Gulf. Galveston Island and this weirdly named building were cosmopolitan by contrast.

As he grew comfortable with me, George made an embarrassed but intrigued inquiry about the other patients he'd seen in the waiting room: "What are they here for?" I told him that I couldn't reveal anything about specific patients, but that the Center's most common requests were for the sex-change surgery that Christine Jorgensen had made famous and the female-to-male equivalent.

The sex-change business resulted in a waiting room filled with people of ambiguous gender who spent the wait for their appointments playing guessing games of who's-going-in-which-direction. A tall thirty-year-old in a tight red minidress and thick pancake makeup, which might conceal beard stubble, would look out from heavily lashed eyes to study the waif of twenty-five in a baseball jersey and cap huddled over pretending to read a dog-eared *Sports Illustrated.* The tall one would abruptly look away as the waif raised big gray eyes for a similar assessment. *Saturday Night Live*'s Pat would have been right at home. They'd probably pegged George as a likely "preop"; pregnancy is not usually an issue for male or female transsexuals.

This exchange about other patients provided an opening for me to ask about George's own sexual orientation and gender identity. The former is used in psychology to describe whom one is attracted to and the latter which gender one feels oneself to be. Surprisingly, these are not always related; men have been known to have sex-change operations to become lesbian.

George's case was not so complicated. "I'm gay. I've been attracted to men as long as I can remember, but I'm not as public about it as the guys in the waiting room." His steady boyfriend of four years had died after a long flulike illness two months before George's false pregnancy began. "Alan was the only serious relationship I'd ever had. Mostly the others had just been people I'd see in gay bars and have sex with. Alan worked in this diner near one construction site. I ate lunch there every day for weeks, and I'd usually bring a mystery novel instead of sitting with the other guys from the crew. It turned out Alan loved mysteries, too. We'd talk about our favorite detectives and recommend books. I thought he was awful cute—kind of boyish looking, with a dark crew cut. I didn't even know for sure if he was gay. You have to be so careful in front of the construction guys, 'cause they'll rag you forever if they know. But one night I went up to Houston to a bar I like, and there was Alan! Seems he'd been wondering the same thing about me. He came home with me that night and moved in two months later. He was such a great guy, quiet like me, so we didn't socialize too much with other people. Any old thing—watching TV, going to the beach—was more fun when he was around. It was almost like we were married or something.

"I miss Alan more than anything. Sometimes I come home from work and just burst into tears because he's not there; he'll never be there waiting for me again. But I think I'm getting better gradually; I'm not as torn up about it as I was the first few weeks."

George described having always thought of himself as a "woman living inside a man's body." He was familiar with the term "transsexual" and identified himself with it, but he had never had any interest in pursuing a sex-change operation. "I've tried dressing up in women's clothes, and I like that, but I only do it occasionally. When I still lived at home with my mother, I'd borrow her things—girdle, bra, dresses. Everything but her shoes fit me, 'cause she's a pretty big woman. Once I was living with Alan, I went to Houston, where no one knew me, and bought a dress—a light blue prom dress. I told the salesgirl it was for my wife. Alan didn't much like to see me in it, but he was an easygoing guy; he never gave me a hard time about it. I kept it in the spare bedroom closet, and I'd put it on every so often when I was home by myself.

"After Alan died, I remember thinking, I wish I really had been a woman so that at least I could have had a child to remember him by." Now his odd symptom seemed not so odd.

When I asked him to sign a release form to permit me to contact Dr. Branden to ask him about the hypnosis, George said, "No way!" It is quite routine to request this of new patients and quite unusual for them to refuse. Even after a lengthy description of how the information could help us, George continued to withhold permission. He explained that he didn't want to look like he was trying to get Dr. Branden into trouble and that he worried the doctor would become angry at him upon learning of the pregnant-woman image. George also said he was afraid that Dr. Branden might insist that he return, rehypnotize him, and take the pregnancy away.

We dispatched a medical student to look up the bit of information about Dr. Branden that was publicly available from the telephone yellow pages and the *Directory of Medical Specialists*. He returned with a report that this physician did exist, did practice hypnosis, and actually listed himself as a general practitioner, although George had described him as a psychiatrist. This was all we were ever able to learn about the original hypnotist and his actions, given George's refusal of a release.

Dr. Branden made a major mistake by not inquiring about his patient's imagery and responses to hypnotic suggestions. This is unfortunately a common problem. A number of hypnotists, especially those who do group hypnosis, never ask about a subject's reactions. The vast majority of the time, people will interpret the suggestions benignly. However, I've heard at least one more alarming example of what can go wrong without inquiry: One hypnotist told a patient to picture himself in a "relaxing place" where he would "put all his troubles aside and feel completely at home" for a number of sessions before discovering that the increasingly suicidal patient was visualizing lying dead in a coffin as his "relaxing place."

In George's case, at no time did he express any clear dislike for the false pregnancy. His voice was calm and almost dreamy when he discussed it. His only real worry was the logistics of a delivery if he were actually pregnant. A conventional heterosexual male visiting Dr. Branden would hardly have developed pseudocyesis.

Now that elaborate physical exams, lab tests, and interviews confirmed that the pregnancy was a phantom, there remained the issue of what to do about it. First, we emphatically told George that he was not pregnant. The physicians explained how the results of his physical were completely incompatible with the hope he seemed to harbor, only half-articulated, that he was some kind of hermaphrodite with female organs hidden away somewhere. Dr. Greer and I supported George's more realistic statements that he could not be pregnant, since the condition had begun with a verbal suggestion, and we commended his ability to relate his previous wish to be pregnant to his current symptoms.

Don Greer, the psychologist for the Gender Disorders Center, was a flamboyant man who liked to say he was "in charge of all kinky sex on the island of Galveston." His office, which I was using to interview George while Dr. Greer came and went from some of his other Center duties, was dominated by a large, baroque desk. Atop it were two tripod stands about six inches high. The one to the left held a crystal-clear Plexiglas sphere encasing a small vampire bat—wings outstretched, fangs bared. On the one to the right sat a shrunken head—real, although I tried to remind myself of the reports that they were now being made from monkey heads.

Dr. Greer's eccentric decor went over well with most of the sex-change candidates. He was outgoing, warm, and had a way of making marginal people feel understood and accepted. George seemed more daunted by his surroundings. He was basically a wholesome, all-American boy except for his wish to be the even more wholesome girl-next-door. Still, he responded to Dr. Greer's warmth and naturalness by confiding to him easily the details of his condition.

George's expectation was that his "pregnancy" would continue for six more months, at which time he would probably, in his words, "experience false labor and then go back to normal." Before I joined the evaluation, Dr. Greer had offered him the option of checking into the hospital and enacting a realistic version of the delivery. I don't know whether he pictured a maternity or psychiatric unit providing this service, but Don Greer was a master at getting the usually conventional hospital staff to do the unheard of, so he probably could have arranged a childbirth scenario. However, George did not take to the idea. When talking to me later, he said, "It's a private thing—like between Alan and me. I hadn't told anybody about my pregnancy until today. I don't think I'd want a bunch of people around. I'd want to be alone with my memories of Alan."

He was equally negative about my first suggestion, which was that I hypnotize him. "We wouldn't have to aim at taking away your false pregnancy. I know that's not what you want right now," I told him. "Hypnosis could be useful in finding out more about why you're having pseudocyesis, when you might be ready to give it up, and finding something better to help you carry a sense of Alan with you. I promise I wouldn't suggest that it go away unless in a future session you decided you were ready for that."

George said no, but he wouldn't really explain his reservations. I think at least partly he didn't trust me enough to accept my assurances. Based on what he'd said about other health providers, it seemed he felt easily controlled.

I was direct with him about the part I was inclined to change immediately: "I don't think the daily visualization is a good idea, at least the way you're doing it now. It's a form of self-hypnosis." I told him that, since there had been so few cases of pseudocyesis in men, no one really knew how the male body produces the physical changes of false pregnancy. It is not by high levels of female hormones. These do exist in trace amounts in the male body, so this hypothesis is not as impossible as it might sound. However, George's lab tests ruled out a hormonal imbalance. Still, his condition wasn't just a matter of posture, thrusting the stomach out the way a man clowning around about being pregnant might; George's abdomen and breasts were actually distended.

Whatever the specific mechanism for pseudocyesis, it is well established that high hypnotizability is related to one's power to alter a wide range of body processes. I've been able to help very hypnotizable people constrict blood vessels and stop profuse bleeding, interrupt severe asthma attacks, and erase the rash of poison ivy within minutes. Studies show the same symptoms can be produced by hypnotic suggestion in the absence of their usual physical triggers. For example, not only did Yale researchers demonstrate that hypnosis suppresses a skin reaction to being rubbed with poison ivy leaves but subjects in a deep trance who were rubbed with rose leaves while being told this was poison ivy developed severe rashes. Most relevant, a study of highly hypnotizable women by Cheryl Wilson and Ted Barber found that a majority of them had experienced the rare disorder of pseudocyesis—and this was without suggestion from formal hypnosis. George's vivid imagery suggested he was quite hypnotizable.

"Even if you could eventually get your body to look nine months pregnant, I don't think that would be good for you," I warned him. I recommended he stop or at least change his visualization: "The relaxation you learned from your smoking cessation is fine, but I wouldn't keep picturing the swollen belly." I suggested there might be an alternative image that could provide a sense that he and Alan had created something special. "One reason I'd like to do the hypnosis with you is that it's a good way to find a substitute." George was interested in this idea and asked me how such a countervisualization might work, but he was still not ready to agree to it. I hoped he would in the future, but I was not going to push further that day.

Dr. Greer rejoined us. I asked George what he wanted to do now and if there was a way we could be of help. "I just want to know for sure if it's a real pregnancy or a false pregnancy."

"It's a false pregnancy!" Dr. Greer and I exclaimed in unison, each for the dozenth time. Given that, was there anything else he wanted from us?

George repeated his plan that he would just continue this way for a while, perhaps as long as six more months, until false labor began. I kept probing to see if I could persuade him to try hypnosis with me in the future. Dr. Greer asked questions subtly biased toward planning a hospitalization for George's future "delivery." We also both entertained the possibility of just letting the process take its course as a reasonable option. The choice was certainly George's to make.

In response to our questions, George described in detail what he expected "labor" to be like. He thought of it as involving a lot of pain, "but pain with a purpose, so you accept it, even welcome it. I've always thought of a woman in labor as feeling agony and ecstasy at the same time." It was clear that his imagery was a metaphor for successful grieving. He proceeded at length, absorbed in his own narration. After describing everything about this experience—presumably to occur six months later—he remarked that he felt his abdomen had suddenly shrunk. This was not dramatically obvious to anyone else, but a bit later we had one of the medical students measure. Sure enough, George's waist was three inches smaller than it had been earlier in the day.

"Maybe that means you'll be ready to complete the process sooner than you'd thought," I told him. Dr. Greer and I both suggested that he go home and consider treatment options. We repeated our assurance that he was most definitely not pregnant one more time as—given his earlier intransigence on the subject—we were suspicious whether that would stick. We asked George to check back with us in two weeks and let us know whether he'd changed his mind about wanting treatment. He agreed and plodded out of the Center. His waddling gait was just as obvious from behind. We were not sure whether we would ever see him, or even hear from him, again.

Hear from him we did, though. He called at his appointed time: "It's all over; I'm not pregnant anymore!" The day after seeing us, George had decided to switch his visualization to something quite ingenious. The image had come from within him as spontaneously as the first vision of a pregnant woman. He abandoned imagining himself pregnant, but, in a similar trancelike state, he began to picture himself as a woman looking back on the experience of labor with a great sense of peace and satisfaction. He had no particular fantasies about a baby, just of having given birth. The imagery was successful; his abdomen was back to normal, and his chest was once again flat and masculine. He wasn't pleased with the latter: "I kind of wish I had kept the breasts; maybe I could get hormone shots. I did two years ago, and I liked them."

Overall, he was glad of the outcome. Although it had been largely his own doing, George was grateful to the hospital staff. "I appreciate your taking this seriously. I was so afraid people would think I was completely crazy if I told them. After talking to you, it turned out just right. And in the last week or so, I'm starting to feel better about Alan. I still miss him, of course, but I can remember some of the great times we had and feel good, too."

Three months later, George called Dr. Greer at the Gender Disorders Center, asking if they could give him estrogen shots like the ones that had given him a sense of well-being two years before. The Center had strict guidelines worked out with the conservative medical school, which had always been dubious about the advisability of the Center's existence. These guidelines allowed estrogen shots for men only as part of a complete protocol for sex change, which began with a year of counseling, a second year of cross-dressing, hair removal, hormone injections, and finally surgery. They could not administer the shots out of protocol, but Dr. Greer gave George the phone number of the Janus Foundation, a national referral service for transsexuality, which would know of private physicians likelier to be receptive to his request.

I never saw George again. His last medical school contact was not with any of the ad hoc false pregnancy evaluation team. I know of it only from his hospital chart. A year and a half after seeing us, George visited the medical unit for evaluation of a persistent sore throat and fatigue, for which his hometown doctor had been unable to find a cause. Their tests were inconclusive also.

George was the only one of my former patients discussed in this book whom I tried to locate and could not. He had vanished without a trace from phone directories of the small area of rural Texas where he had lived all his life. His young homosexual partner's death in 1979 from a prolonged, flulike illness and his own similar complaints in 1981 triggered no alarm bells at that time. But in retrospect, I fear that they may have belonged to the first wave of what is now a grimly familiar disease and that George may have joined Alan prematurely. I hope that I am wrong and that he lives in some other part of the country, perhaps one more hospitable to a gay lifestyle, in a satisfying new relationship and at ease with the conundrums of gender.

5
The Noisy Ghost

From the first words of her initial phone call, Marie presented me with a steady stream of small reminders that the most probable explanation is not necessarily the correct one. "Can hypnosis help you remember something you've repressed?" she asked.

This query usually comes from someone suspecting childhood sexual abuse. Ellen Bass and Laura Davis suggested in their 1988 book, *The Courage to Heal,* that if you wonder whether you have been sexually abused, you probably have. Ironically, the increased publicity about abuse resulting from such pronouncements has probably rendered them less accurate. In the era of secrecy, few other things would have raised such suspicions; much would have conspired to suppress them. By the time of my 1994 conversation, the media was constantly raising the question and *many* people were wondering.

"Yes, sometimes hypnosis can help," I replied cautiously. "What is it that you are trying to remember?"

"Six months ago my sister Chris died . . . she shot herself. I was the one who found her body. That was about eleven o'clock at night. I don't remember anything until around ten-thirty the next morning, even though I was up talking to people a lot of the time." This was not the routine request for hypnotic memory work. Amnesia for events of adulthood is rarer than that for childhood.

"Why do you want to remember the details of her death?"

"I haven't gotten over her suicide. I mean, it's really driving me crazy. I haven't been working. I saw a counselor and that didn't help. Recently I've been having these nightmares and I can't sleep."

"What are the nightmares about?"

"It's really this one dream that I keep having over and over about a woman named Chris—not my sister—trying to kill me. I hardly sleep now. There's . . . uh . . . other stuff happening, too," she added cryptically. "I'll tell you about it if you agree to see me."

"Well, hypnosis can often aid memory, but there may be a reason that you're repressing it. People often feel worse at first after recalling something traumatic."

"I know I'd feel awful, but I think it would help me start getting over it." This seemed like a realistic expectation. I gave her an appointment for the following Monday.

I have never seen an adult exhibit such extreme amnesia unless there was an early childhood history of trauma through which he or she learned repression as a defense. Some theorists believe that it is only possible for the brain to develop dissociative tendencies in childhood, while it is growing and organizing itself. However, the literature on battlefield psychology is full of reports of sudden memory losses in adults who were not known to have any previous psychiatric disturbance. It is possible that the small percentage of soldiers who respond to the horror of war by dissociating it have an unknown history of childhood trauma. Recognizing it would be rash to assume this merely to bolster a theory, I kept an open mind on the topic. I wondered if Marie would be the first patient I'd see who genuinely experienced amnesia for the first time as an adult.

In addition to my study of trauma and hypnosis, I had done research on dreams after bereavement. Most of these represent simple grief or an attempt to reverse or deny the loss. However, a common class of bereavement dreams depicts a summons from the grave in which the dead reach out, imploring or grabbing the living to join them. The most macabre ones in my study came from three college students who were keeping dream journals in the wake of a classmate's suicide. Their dreams ranged from seeing her wink in a sinister way from her coffin to having her get up and pursue them. My caller's recurring nightmare might be fueled by such dynamics.

Marie was a slight young woman with the glossy black hair typical of her Italian heritage. She told me she was twenty-four; I would have guessed younger. Her childlike

prettiness, wide blue eyes, and deferential manner reminded me of my patient Nancy from fifteen years earlier.
She fidgeted, seemingly unable to feel at ease in the con-
sultation room. Nancy, the daughter of an academic physician, had seemed more at home with therapy. Marie told
me her father had been a career army officer until his
death from a heart attack four years before. "We moved
around a lot until I was eleven. I could never make really
close friends 'cause I always had to leave them behind. My
sister Chris was my best friend. She was just a year older
than me."

"Do you have other sisters or brothers?" I asked.

"Uh huh. I have a younger sister, Joyce, and an older
brother, Joe."

"Are you close to them?"

"Oh, yeah. We all live in two duplexes. Mom and
Grandma are upstairs in one building, and Joyce's in the
lower unit. Then me and Chr"—she stopped herself—"me
and Joe and my son, Timmie, live in the duplex next
door."

"How old is Timmie?"

"He just turned six."

"Is Timmie's father around?"

"Nope," she replied without volunteering further details. "Things were really good until two years ago. Chris
was in the army reserves, and she got sent overseas for
Operation Desert Storm. She came back upset about
things she'd seen. She wasn't in the fighting, but she was
in one of the helicopters that did body counts after the retreat. She felt really guilty somehow. She never did tell me
everything. She said she was glad I'd never have to see
those things. She always looked out for me like that.

When she came back, she hung around with her friends from the reserves more, and she drank a lot. I don't drink at all; I'm kind of against it. But I never thought she'd do this . . . and I can't even remember."

"Why don't you tell me what you do remember?"

"I was really sick that night. I was in bed with a temperature. A friend called, and I talked to her awhile. After I hung up, I must have fallen asleep soon. I remember waking up and thinking that I'd heard a door slam downstairs. Now I wonder if it was the gun. Then, I just figured it was the front door and Chris was home. I thought I should go down and check on her 'cause half the time she was drunk when she came in. But I was just too sick, and I guess I went to sleep again. The next thing I remember is somebody pounding on my door. At first I thought it was my boyfriend, Chuck, and I wasn't going to answer it. Then I could hear a bunch of people yelling. I got up and went to the door. Four of Chris's army friends were there. They said they'd knocked on Chris's door and no one answered. They were worried about her 'cause she was real down when they dropped her off earlier. They wanted me to let them into her place. I sent them down the outside steps to her front door while I took the inside steps to her apartment. I called 'Chris,' and there was no answer. I walked into her bedroom. That's all I remember. I mean, I know some of the other things that happened, but that's all I actually recall myself."

"And what else do you know from what people have told you?"

"Well, I know she was dead in her bed. She'd put her army pistol in her mouth and shot herself. I was the one who made the 911 call. They told me I said my sister had killed herself and I gave the address and all. I guess I was pretty hysterical by the end of the call. Last month, I tried to get the police to let me listen to the tape to see if it would jog my memory. They said no, I was really screaming at the end, and it would upset me too much.

"Anyway, by the time Chris's friends were inside and the ambulance came, I was calm. I talked to the ambulance people and told them which funeral home our family used. I called my mother and grandmother, who were at this lake in New Hampshire where they go every year. I called Chris's boyfriend and other people to tell them. I put Timmie to bed in his room. Chuck stayed, and we went to bed in my room. I don't remember any of this. And, the thing that really gets to me is this—Chuck woke up at five and I wasn't there. He thought I was next door at my sister Joyce's, but it turned out I wasn't. Joyce came to my house at eight, and I didn't show up until ten-thirty. I have no idea where I was or what I was doing."

"Have you had any more periods that you can't remember since then?"

"No."

"What about before your sister's death? Had you ever had amnesia in the past?"

"No." As I've indicated earlier, such memory loss would be very unusual, so I questioned Marie about things potentially related to developing childhood dissociation.

"Did you ever have any really bad, traumatic things happen to you when you were a child?"

"No, our family was always the happiest on the block. My dad did drink a bit too much, but it was a great family." I was not sure whether to take this statement at face

value. I've had two people tell me that they had very
happy childhoods but didn't remember anything before
the age of eighteen, when they left home. Both turned out
to have had horrific histories. However, Marie's assurance
was emphatic enough that to question it more at this point
might have damaged our rapport.

"No other traumas since you've been an adult?"

"Well . . ." She hesitated, then volunteered in a casual
voice, "I did find someone else dead in Chris's bed two
years ago."

Huh? "Who?"

"Gillian, this friend of hers from New York, was visiting. Chris let her sleep in the bedroom, and Chris took the
living room couch. I came down that morning looking for
Chris and went into the bedroom. There was Gillian, lying
in bed with her eyes open, staring. She'd died of a heart
attack even though she was only thirty-one. It turned out
she had a congenital heart condition. But that wasn't traumatic; I didn't know her. Except afterwards we thought
Chris's house was haunted. The TV would come on, and
there would be noises like . . . well . . . I don't want to get
into that now." She quickly shifted gears. "Let me tell you
about the nightmare I keep having. That's the worst thing
right now."

"Yes, you mentioned it on the phone."

"In the dream this other Chris is trying to kill me. The
details are always different. Sometimes she has a knife,
other times a gun. She may be breaking in through my
window, or sometimes she's already in the house, walking into my room. I always wake up just before she's going to get me."

"I'm not sure I understand," I said. "Is this a real-life

person you know named Chris or is the dream character a stranger who has your sister's name?"

"This is a real-life Chris, my brother Joe's ex-girlfriend."

"What kind of person is she?" This Chris might well have been just a stand-in for the sister, cast in the dream mostly for her name, but I wanted to check out her personal importance.

"She's crazy and mean. That's why Joe broke up with her, and she's gotten even crazier and meaner since he did."

"Can you describe what she does that's crazy and mean?"

"Well, she threatened to kill me," Marie replied hesitantly, as if she wasn't quite sure this qualified. Now it was obvious that more than her name determined this Chris's presence in the dream.

"Why did she want to kill you?"

"My brother moved in with me when they broke up. Chris—the ex-girlfriend—thinks Chris—my sister—and I talked him into it. She thinks we're too close. She accused us of incest, actually. The first time she called, she said she was going to kill Chris and me. Then after Chris was dead, this other Chris called up and said, 'Your sister killed herself. She deserved to die and you do too.'"

"I certainly see why you say she's mean and crazy. Do you have any reason to think she could really be violent?"

"She did try to run my brother over with a car," Marie offered, in the same minimalist tone. "He got a few bruises, and he was treated at the hospital and released."

"And you wonder why you're having nightmares about her?"

"Well, things don't usually get to me."

"Is your house secure? Do you think you need to take any precautions to protect yourself from this woman?"

"The house is pretty burglarproof. I just don't feel safe now that Chris's gone. She used to protect me from everything."

"From people trying to kill you?" I tended to assume the security afforded by an older sister was more emotional than physical.

"Well, yes. Timmie's father was a pretty bad guy. After I broke up with him, he kept saying he'd kill me if I didn't take him back. One day after church, he came up to me right in front of the church with Timmie and everything. He started hassling me and when I tried to leave, he hit me. He knocked me to the sidewalk and kicked me. I blacked out; later I had a concussion. He just walked away. People from the church came down and called an ambulance. They had to pull Timmie out of the street where he was trying to stop cars.

"My family wasn't at church 'cause Mom's rheumatism was acting up, and Chris and Joe stopped going years ago. When they got called, they all came and stayed with me at the hospital except Chris. She went and got a baseball bat and went to Timmie's father's apartment. He was there, and she just started beating on him, saying, 'You should never have done that to Marie.' He had several broken bones and a dislocated shoulder. She told him if he ever came near me again she'd kill him. He must have believed her 'cause he hasn't."

"That's quite a story. A few minutes ago, you told me nothing else traumatic had ever happened to you as an adult."

"Well, I guess I wasn't thinking about him. But after that it was okay. When Chris was alive, things couldn't get too bad." Obviously Marie was right that her sister's suicide had devastated her like nothing previously, so I returned to that topic.

"You said there were other things bothering you connected to Chris's death."

"Timmie's started talking about her in weird ways."

"Like how?"

"Well, a couple weeks ago he wanted to show me that he could do a cartwheel. He led me out to the backyard and did two perfect ones on the grass. I told him that was wonderful and asked where he'd learned how. He said, 'Aunt Chris showed me.'

"I said, 'But Aunt Chris's dead,' and he sort of clammed up. I couldn't get him to say if he meant she'd showed him a long time ago and he'd just figured out how to do it himself or what.

"Then he was talking about the Red Sox and Mo Vaughn's home run. We hadn't had the game on. I asked who told him 'cause he couldn't read the paper yet. He said Aunt Chris did. Maybe he'd heard it on TV or from one of his friends, but I couldn't get any more out of him.

"A few days later, he was talking on the phone when I walked in. He said, 'I got to go,' and put the phone down real fast. I asked him who it was and he said, 'Aunt Chris.' I don't know if there even was anyone on the other end. He could have been talking to one of his friends—they call each other now. Or he could have been having a pretend conversation with Chris without having dialed at all."

"Does Timmie seem unhappy? Has he been having any other problems since Chris's death?"

"No, I've been surprised. Right after she died, he would ask why she couldn't come back. When he understood that, he'd say he wished she wasn't dead. Then some of the older kids at school had to start in on him about how his aunt killed herself. We'd told him it was an accident—that's what the papers said too—but he came home asking all these questions about suicide. I told him that suicide was a kind of accident. That she shot herself, but she was too drunk to know she didn't want to do that. I said she wouldn't have wanted to leave us if she knew what she was doing." Marie teared up and blinked rapidly.

She composed herself and continued, "He seems fine now. I asked his teacher and she says he's well adjusted and doing well in all his subjects. He has lots of friends. He seems fine to me except for saying those things."

"Is there something else yet bothering you since Chris's death? Several times you started to tell me something and then stopped. Like when you were talking about Gillian."

"Yeah. I . . . uh . . . hear a sound like gunshot. It's like after Gillian died. Sometimes I just hear it. Sometimes at the same time something moves."

"Like what?"

"One time it was her hairbrush—well, the one I use now. It just went flying across the room. I find things moved from where I put them a lot. And the TV just comes on without anyone turning it on. Usually I'm somewhere else in the house, but twice I've been in the room with it. I even took the set to the repair shop. They couldn't find anything wrong with it.

"I was really scared when I thought Gillian was haunting us 'cause maybe she was a bad spirit. Now when those things happen I just say, 'Hello, Chris. I know you're here.'"

What Marie was describing was classic for a poltergeist, the German phrase meaning "noisy ghost," made popular by the movie of the same title. Poltergeists are often associated with explosive noises, if not actual gunshots. Unlike the film's literal ghost explanation, parapsychologists, professional students of the paranormal, note that the disturbances often center on a hysterical young woman. The leading parapsychology theory is that the upset woman uses unconscious telekinesis, or the movement of objects through thought alone, and that ghosts play no role.

Obviously, there were less mysterious explanations for some of what Marie reported. It didn't seem surprising that in a house with a six-year-old, objects were often not where she had left them. As for the noises and movements, it was not impossible for a sane, highly hypnotizable person to see such things. I had no explanation for her sister Chris also witnessing the phenomena after Gillian died, but otherwise what Marie described was not unlike Nancy's hallucinations of lights and stereos malfunctioning. However, my explanations were less important than Marie's perspective.

"How do you understand it—what do you think is going on?"

"I think Chris is around in some way. I believe that ghosts or spirits are possible, although I don't understand how they work."

Despite my skepticism, I kept my tone neutral so as

not to influence Marie's answer. "Do you think your son is talking to Chris's ghost?"

Marie frowned with perplexity. "I think of his stuff more like he's imagining it. I guess I think it's possible, though. That's part of why I try to ask him more about it. Maybe it's not fair to think of it as imaginary when it's him and real when it's me. They say children see more."

"Do all these strange sounds and movements happen in your place or Chris's?"

"I live in her place now. I was sleeping there every night anyway, so I just moved in along with Timmie and let Joe have mine. I left my furniture for him since I kept all Chris's stuff. People tell me I should change it, but I don't want to. I love her things. I did finally take the head-board off the bed 'cause I couldn't get the blood out of the wood grain. I've put my clothes in the closets, but hers are there, too. We're the same size, and we always wore each other's things anyway."

Our time was getting short, so I asked the mandatory question of a new patient as depressed as Marie. "Do you have any thoughts about killing yourself?"

"Yeah, I think about it a lot," she said. "But I would never let myself do it because of Timmie." This answer was fairly typical. Besides depression, a number of factors play a role in suicidality. Being the mother of a young child is the single best predictor against suicide. Being Catholic correlates with a lower risk. Chris had been stricken with the most ominous predictor for depressives following through on suicide—alcoholism—while Marie didn't drink.

I did not judge Marie to be a serious suicide risk, but it was alarming how identified she was with her dead sister. She was living in Chris's apartment, sleeping in the bed she died in, wearing her clothes, dreaming of imminent death, and hearing gunshot noises. She had been grieving her sister's death for almost the same amount of time as George had mourned his partner, Alan. Despite his symptom of the phantom pregnancy, George had gotten on with the rest of his life. His attempt to hang on to Alan was consolidated in that one symbol. Marie's need to hang on to Chris was determining every aspect of her existence. She described a sense of being haunted. It seemed to me more that she was haunting Chris's life than the other way around.

I used our remaining time to ask Marie a few questions about her ability to use imagery and ascertained that she was likely to be highly hypnotizable. I told her we could do the hypnosis in the next session if she was still sure she wanted to.

"I want to, but can I bring my sister Joyce?"

"You mean in the room to watch?"

"Yeah," she said apologetically, sensing I didn't like the idea.

Since my first experience with Hunter's impromptu trance, I have been leery of hypnotic observers. I also thought it unwise to have a family member in the room with Marie since I could not be sure of the content if she remembered the missing time.

"Watching hypnosis is not such a good idea. Why do you want her here?"

"In case I say things that I can't remember later."

I advised Marie that the odds were overwhelming that anything she remembered in a trance, she would also remember upon awakening. I also offered to take notes or make a tape just in case. She liked the idea of a tape.

"Okay, but if you don't remember because there's something really upsetting on the tape, I can't just hand it to you," I told her. "We'd have to work in more sessions at getting you ready to be aware of what's on it. Is that acceptable?"

"Yeah. That makes sense. Can I still bring Joyce with me, just to sit in the waiting room? In case I don't feel like driving myself home?"

"That would be fine." We made an appointment for Friday.

Joyce was a pleasant and attractive young woman—a happier, even younger version of Marie. Despite her friendly demeanor, I got the sense that she was subtly checking out whether I was good for her sister.

"I hope this helps," Joyce told me. "She hasn't been herself since Chris died. She quit her job. She broke up with her boyfriend and doesn't see any of her old friends except Chris's boyfriend."

"It's not like we're dating or anything," Marie interjected indignantly. "We just like to hang out and talk about her."

"I know. That's what I mean. She's even talking about joining the army. Although it's not like she's going to get it together to go down there anytime soon, she stays in her house so much. It's like we lost both of them."

I settled Joyce in the waiting room and offered her some magazines. She took them and thanked me. However, I doubted she would read any of them. Her real mission seemed to be to stand guard. I retreated into my office with Marie and closed the door.

Marie was anxious but eager to begin. She picked the couch for hypnosis. I plucked a new blank audiocassette from a package I keep in the office mostly for making my patients' self-hypnosis tapes. I laid its plastic case on the desk chair and put the tape in the recorder. I moved the machine down to the chair beside the empty case so that its microphone cord would reach across the room.

To be in a position to record, I sat in the armchair at the head of the couch. This is where Freud sat when doing analysis, but closer than I usually am. Generally, I reserve this chair and the couch as my patient's seating choices, and I sit in the desk chair, six feet away. This is close enough for communication but gives my post-traumatic stress patients the distance they need—many of them are vigilant and territorial. In this session, however, I needed to hold the microphone close to Marie's head.

I asked her to close her eyes. "I want you to begin to relax your body, starting with the muscles of your feet and toes," I suggested. I talked her through the usual relaxation sequence. I was careful not to use walking down a staircase as the deepening visualization, since I knew that image played a role in the devastating events we were going to explore. Instead I talked about waves of relaxation moving through her body. After a little while, she appeared to be deep in trance.

"Now, I want you to turn your attention to your sister Chris," I began.

A sharp *pop* issued from somewhere to my right, and
I looked over just in time to see the empty cassette case
fly across the room and land with a *plop* on the rug at the
foot of the couch. My stomach went cold. I looked back
at Marie, who continued to lie still, eyes closed, utterly relaxed, apparently not having reacted to the sound at all.

I still write myself notes about what I am going to do
in a session. In student days, I used to consult them; now
the act of writing fixes the content in my memory. However, for the first time in fifteen years, I looked down at
them, having gone utterly blank as to my next intended
step. I found my place. "You can begin moving back in
time," I intoned, fixing my gaze mostly on Marie but
sneaking looks back at the plastic cassette case lying on
the floor and the empty place next to the tape recorder on
the chair. Suddenly it mattered very much to me whether
or not there was a physical explanation for these phenomena.

I set the stage, gradually moving Marie back into her
house on the night of her sister's death. She tensed somewhat. I was still half-expecting another explosive sound,
but gradually I became focused on what we were doing.
"You're in bed talking to your friend. You finish and hang
up the phone." I was feeding back to her what she had
told me during the previous session. Now I was able to
work without the notes again. "You turn out the lamp to
go to sleep. Can you feel yourself in the scene?"

"Yeah, I lie in the dark." Marie took over the narration
without prompting. "I'm feverish; I'm dozing. There's a
bang. I think I heard the front door slam. Chris's home. I
should go down. I'm too tired. I'm dozing again. The
doorbell rings. I don't answer. It must be my boyfriend,

Chuck. I don't feel like seeing him tonight. The bell keeps on ringing, and people are banging on the door, too. I go to the door and four of her friends are there. 'It's about Chris,' one says.

" 'Was she in a car accident?' I ask. They say she's in the house, they brought her home an hour ago and want to check on her. I go through my house to the back stairs and go down into her place. The lights are on." Marie bit her lip and her breathing quickened. "I call her name. I go into the bedroom.

"She's lying in bed. I see her gun. I don't even know if it was on her or beside her. I just focus on this gun lying on its side. She's bleeding from her mouth and her ears. I back up against the wall. She's just lying there with her eyes closed. She looks like an angel. Her face is so peaceful except for the blood flowing out to the sides. A scream is coming out of me. I can't stop it." Marie looked quite distraught now and did not immediately continue talking. I suggested that she could remain calm and tell me what happened next. She did relax significantly.

"I back out of the room and go upstairs yelling. Chris's friends are in my apartment now. They hear me tell 911 my sister just shot herself. They head down her stairs. Joe comes out of his room; he doesn't know what's happened. Then Timmie comes. 'Put him back in his room! Don't let him go down there!' " Marie's tone changed to urgency as she moved into the scene completely for a moment. "Joe takes him back in. I keep talking to the 911 lady, telling her the address. She says, 'Stay calm,' and somehow that makes me completely lose it. I'm just shrieking and hand the phone to Joe when he comes out of Timmie's room. I'm not sure he even knows who he's talking to. He says,

'I guess something happened to my sister Chris,' but I hear him repeating the address and telling her about the Dunkin' Donuts on the corner where you turn, so I go back downstairs. I want to go in to her. Her friends won't let me. 'I'll stop yelling.' " Again Marie's voice changed as she seemed to plead with Chris's friends, " 'I just want to go in there. I want to hold her.' This guy grabs me and hugs me but he won't let me through the door.

"I go outside and around to Joyce's house. I beat on her door. I don't hear anything at first. I keep banging and eventually she's there. 'Chris's dead,' I say. 'What happened?' she asks me and I can't answer. She holds me and I sob. She starts crying. Eventually I manage to say she shot herself. 'When?' 'Just now.' Joyce comes back toward my house holding my hand. There's an ambulance outside now and two police cars. Just as we get in front, a news van pulls up and a reporter with a video camera jumps out and she asks if we know the woman who shot herself. Joyce yells to go away and I'm cursing. I grab at the camera, but she gets it away from me. The police come and tell everyone that they need to back up to the sidewalk. They're putting yellow tape around our yard. I sit on the front steps. Someone's called Chuck, and he shows up. He's trying to comfort me. I don't want him around right now. I say, 'Go in and check on Timmie for me, will you? Make sure he's okay.' Chuck goes in the house. People are gathering—lots of neighbors and more reporters. Little Susie Adams comes from a play dressed in a mermaid outfit with two boys in sailors' suits. The press tries to ask them questions about Chris." Marie's monologue was so evocative that for a moment I felt as if I were behind the scenes of one of those tasteless news reports I've seen so often, where shell-shocked relatives repeat "No comment" blankly to the television camera.

"The coroner's truck maneuvers around. They ask me to stand out of the way. I try to go back inside, a policeman blocks me. They roll her out. She's under a blanket. They take her past me into the truck. I'm yelling, 'Chris! No, don't take her! Chris!' The policeman's holding me back." Marie's lip quivered and tears rolled down her cheeks for the first time in the session. "They want me to go upstairs; eventually I do."

Her voice calmed again as she continued her narrative. "Chris's four friends and Joyce are standing in the living room. They tell me it was an accident. I look at them like they're crazy. 'It couldn't have been.' They say, 'Well, that's what we're telling the press. They want a statement. Don't say any different.' I say, 'Fine, I'm not talking to the press anyway.' "

Listening to Marie, I saw everything she described. Although I could direct her when I needed to, I was almost in a light trance myself. I had the illusion of experiencing her account in real time. Actually, however, it had taken her fifteen minutes to recount about an hour of the tragedy. We had time for the whole night in this session. Marie described a long string of visits and calls. She phoned her mother and grandmother in New Hampshire and broke the news. She called Chris's boyfriend's house and got his brother who was peculiarly hard to convince that she was serious. He finally agreed to find his brother. Marie also notified a myriad of lesser acquaintances and relatives. As the news rippled through the tight neighborhood, friends hurried over. The house was full into the wee hours of the morning. When people finally left, Tim-

mie was long asleep. The rest of the family went to bed—
Joe in his room. Chuck insisted on staying with Marie.

"I wait until he's asleep. I leave him a note saying, 'I'm
fine. I'll be back.' I go downstairs. Everything's dark. I turn
on a light and go right for her bedroom. I get in the bed.
Someone's changed the sheets. There's no blood except
for the headboard. There's a bullet hole through it and
bloodstains are traced into the grain of the wood. I pull
the covers up. I feel really comfortable. It's warm, like
she's still here. I start to doze. I hear a sound that scares
me, it sounds like a gun going off. I walk into the parlor.
The answering machine catches my eye. I press the play
button. The first message has her voice. She's drunk,
sounds so sad. She tells them she's okay. Donna's on the
phone with her. Then a message from one of her army
friends who I don't know. 'Chris, you're scaring me. Won't
you answer the phone or door? I hope you're not answering the phone because you're sleeping.' The next one
is Mom: 'I'm calling from New Hampshire. It's your god-
damn mother, pick up the fucking phone.' " Marie's voice
distorted nastily as she imitated this. I wondered again
about her happy childhood.

"The curtains start to blow. I feel so lost. It doesn't feel
like she's there anymore. I go to Joyce's, but she's not in.
She must have spent the rest of the night at her
boyfriend's. I'm in Chris's room again for a moment but it
doesn't feel like she's there anymore. I take her army ring.
I put it on my finger and go to the funeral home. It's a
long way but I don't take the car, I walk." Marie narrated
the route and her arrival at the mortuary.

"It's not really open, but there's staff there. They remember me from Dad's funeral. They don't want me to go

in there. She's not ready, they say. They have her in a coffin, but they haven't made her up. I tell her they shouldn't—she didn't wear makeup. I give them the ring and tell them she would have wanted to be buried wearing it. I sit waiting. Someone tells me I should go home and come back later. But the director lets me go in."

"Oh, Chris." Marie gasped, her tone between pain and awe. "She looks so peaceful. But they've got her hair all funny. They have it fluffed up; that's not how she wears it. I start combing her hair. I want to make her perfect. Her lips were burned, I put pink on her lips; I used my lipstick." Marie switched to the past tense when she wasn't as directly reliving the scene. "I just sat there for a long time and kissed her and told her I missed her and loved her. They brought me her bracelet and earrings and old me to take them unless I wanted her buried in them. I said, no, just the ring. I took them. One of her earrings still had blood on it, right over the lily of the valley flower." Marie's right ear was in my view. I saw the design she was describing dangling from her lobe.

"What happened next?"

"I leave. When I get home, Mom's there. She and Grandma just drove back from New Hampshire. She asks me, 'Why, why would she do that?' "

" 'I don't know, Mommy.' Timmie comes in and wants to lie down on my bed. I'm lying with Timmie telling him he can take a nap, and instead, I go to sleep."

"Is there anything else there to remember?" I asked, meaning that morning, but she jumped to the next day.

"We're all at the cemetery. They've just said a prayer. I hear a gunshot. And another." Marie flinched. "I know it's a military salute, but no one told me there'd be shots." Her voice was plaintive. "How could they do that?"

I didn't know quite what to make of her reliving now parts of the days for which she had not reported amnesia. I was aware of our time running short but Marie continued. "They're lowering her into the ground now. When I see the coffin going down, I'm frightened. It feels like there's a hand pulling me, like I'm going to drown." She shuddered. "Then I shake that feeling off and I'm just terribly sad." She was quiet.

"Is that all?"

Marie nodded. I counted her back from ten to one after giving her the suggestion that she would remember "all of these events that you are ready to, clearly and in detail when you wake up."

"Did you get everything on tape?" she asked immediately upon opening her eyes. Only then did I remember the cassette case, which was still lying on the rug across the room.

"I think so, I'll make sure," I said as I pressed the rewind button. "How much do you recall?"

"I remember everything, but I still want to listen to the tape." I stopped near the beginning and hit the play button. It caught the end of my induction loud and clear, despite the usual reel noise of my small recorder.

"Now I want you to turn your attention to your sister Chris," said the recorder. Then came a *pop* but it was faint above the background hiss. The microphone had been close to me and far from the chair. Marie did not react to the noise. I was preoccupied with it again, but I didn't feel it was relevant to my patient's concerns at the moment. As her voice began on the tape, it was softer than mine but audible. "I lie in the dark. I'm feverish." I turned the recorder off.

"Those two moments from the funeral at the end—do you know why you recalled them just now?"

"Those were two other things I didn't remember, or at least I hadn't thought about them since that day."

"Can you tell me a little more about that feeling of being pulled down toward the earth?"

"There's a pull, like I'm going to be buried." Marie automatically switched to the present tense again. Her eyes were open but she looked like she was going back into a slight trance. "I can't breathe, a hand reaches out to grab me. I feel like I'm going to drown." Although this could be read as a metaphor of grief over Chris and longing to be with her, the concreteness of Marie's body sensations sounded like the memory of a real trauma to me. Clinicians treating trauma have long noted the tendency for traumatic memories to be stored as vivid sensory impressions—pain, smell, a distinctive sound, a horrific visual image—that have resisted being processed into more abstract verbal memories. Recently Bessel van der Kolk and a team of researchers at Harvard Medical School have demonstrated this with brain scans; when traumatized patients are asked to recall the trauma, the areas of their brains associated with sensory images and intense emotions are activated. By contrast, when people recall significant but nontraumatic events, their language centers are activated.

"Have you ever really come close to suffocation or drowning?" I asked.

"I did almost drown once, but I don't want to talk about that now," she said, her trancelike demeanor gone.

I didn't push. She'd reexperienced more than enough tragedies for today. I asked about her wishes concerning future sessions, encouraging her to come back to work through what we had uncovered. She agreed to meet again in a week to work on getting a sense of closure, but she reiterated that she didn't want to be in therapy after that. We called Joyce into the room.

"I remembered," Marie announced before Joyce had time to ask the obvious question. "It was okay, really sad, but nothing bad that I didn't already know."

"Where were you in the morning when we couldn't find you?"

"I was at the funeral home. The manager let me in early. I was just sitting with her. I'm glad I can remember that part."

Joyce looked at me. "I hope she's going to get better now. We've been so worried about her. She and Chris were always the closest ones in the family." As Joyce said this, I glimpsed what a complex issue this must be for her. If the other two sisters were the closest, she as the remaining girl must have felt somewhat excluded. Now, through tragedy, her next oldest sister was more hers, but Joyce was playing the caretaking role. Still, I wasn't going to get to know even Marie well, and I wouldn't learn any more of Joyce's place in this strange family.

I took the tape out of the recorder. I stepped over and retrieved the empty case from the floor. Neither of them questioned this as I placed the tape inside and handed it to Marie.

After they left, Chris haunted me. The vivid enactment of her suicide left me wondering why she did it. I also found myself glancing at the empty desk chair and the remaining tapes on the desk, half-expecting another strange sound.

I have heard my share of supernatural anecdotes—not so much in the course of hypnosis, as while pursuing my other specialty, dreamwork. Mysterious coincidences have an affinity for dreams. The explanatory theories from parapsychologists I'd read struck me as silly—circular, explaining nothing. On the other hand, the common "scientific" stance of simply ignoring data that can't be explained by any existing theory is actually quite unscientific. The real explanation was either something not yet discovered or actually just coincidence. Perhaps when a one-in-a-million coincidence seems impossible it's because we don't notice the nine hundred ninety-nine thousand plus times that such outcomes don't happen. One thing is clear—these things certainly affect us profoundly when they do occur. I gradually refocused on the perspective I'd had when Marie first reported the noises: that they were not that important compared with her grief and whether she would be able to detach herself from her sister's life.

I was worried when I checked my answering machine between sessions six days later and found a message from Marie. "I can't come tomorrow. I'm sorry. A lot of stuff has happened. I'll call you and reschedule another time." She hadn't phoned again after three days, so I left a message for her indicating that I would keep the same time open the following week. I asked her to let me know if she wanted that appointment. Her schedule as she had described it in our initial meeting wasn't busy—she was unemployed, and Timmie was at school much of the day. Not hearing from her promptly, I wondered if she was avoiding any follow-up to sort through the memory she'd retrieved. However, she telephoned a day before the proffered appointment to confirm.

"My friend Chris called," she told me when she got to the session. "Remember, the one I told you about?" For a second I thought only of the dead sister allegedly phoning Timmie. Marie had hardly referred to the other Chris as a "friend" before, so it took me a minute to place the nightmare assailant who in waking life had tried to run over her brother, Joe.

"Uh, yes," I replied hesitantly, "I remember."

"Well, she called up and said she was going to kill herself. That she had a bottle of sleeping pills, had already taken ten of them, and was going to take the rest. She was all hysterical about how nobody liked her. I told her to hang on and went up to Joe's apartment and had him call 911 while I went back to keep her talking. An ambulance got to her place while she was still on the phone with me. They took her to the hospital, and she was admitted to the psych ward. Her four-year-old son didn't have anyone else to stay with, so I ended up looking after him for nine days till she got out."

"I thought you and she were more like enemies."

"When she called, she said I was the only one she could talk to. I think she's driven all her friends away."

"How do you feel about her now?"

Marie paused thoughtfully before answering. "Like I saved the wrong one. If I could stop her from killing herself, why not Chris?" She blinked back a tear and continued. "But I guess I did the right thing. I feel sorry for her.

She's pretty messed up. And her son is really sweet. It was nice for Timmie to have him around 'cause he just worships Timmie. You know that age where any boy a couple years older is a supercool dude." As Marie said this, a smile played on her face—the first one I had seen.

"How has everything else been since I saw you?"

"The nightmares stopped." It was hard to guess whether the hypnosis had accomplished this. It might have helped that the person she was dreaming about trying to kill her was both friendlier *and* locked up. "I've been out with my old friends a couple times. Everything else is better now, except I have this new problem. I used to visit Chris's grave every day. Now when I go to the cemetery, I get the feeling that I'm being pulled down or suffocating, like in the hypnosis. I haven't been able to make myself go to the cemetery at all this week."

Intuition led me to ask, "Who else is buried there?"

"My father and my grandparents on his side. Then some distant relatives who I never really knew." Her casual vagueness diminished my sense that there was something to this line of questioning, and I reverted to my previous hypothesis that she was experiencing a sensation analogous to the pull-from-the-grave dreams that I have mentioned. The bereaved may be ambivalent about surviving their loved ones. After projecting their impulse to join them, they can react to it with fear.

"Maybe we should explore that feeling in the hypnosis today as well as the other things we've talked about needing closure."

Marie agreed. She settled herself on the couch, and I went through a hypnotic induction. I did not use the tape recorder this time. All was silent in the vicinity of the desk.

"Focus on your sister Chris," I said. "Tell her you want to say good-bye. Can you see her?"

"Yeah, she's sitting cross-legged on the floor. She looks like she did in junior high—kind of tomboyish and carefree."

"Can you talk to her?"

"Yeah, she's speaking. She says, 'It was a mistake like you said—the bad parts took over.' She tells me I shouldn't imitate her bad habits, I can be the best of both of us. She's talking about Timmie and how he needs me and he's going to grow up to be a wonderful man.

" 'You can move things around, you know,' Chris says. 'It's your house now.' I see a different version of it, still mostly her furniture but there's my dining table I've always loved. Some of my show posters are on the walls. They always used to cheer me up. And we've put up some of Timmie's pictures. He's a good artist. He draws all these bright science fiction things and he loves to show them off.

"She smiles and says, 'You're no soldier, Madame Curie.' " Marie paused for a while and I puzzled over that name until she spoke again. "I love you, too." Apparently she was answering Chris's side of dialogue.

"Do you want to say good-bye?" I asked.

"No, it's like she's still here but I can go on anyway." I retreated from the plan of a more complete separation, which was obviously my agenda, not Marie's.

"Okay. Now we can explore the other image. Let the conversation with Chris fade from your mind's eye as you keep resting and relaxing. Next you can turn your attention to the feeling you have when you're in the cemetery. Can you see yourself standing by your family plot?"

"Yes."

"Can you feel the pull toward Chris's grave?"

"No," she corrected me. "I'm being pulled toward my father's grave. There's a hand, and I'm drowning."

"Are there any other images that reminds you of?" I asked, knowing that even awake she had real-life associations with drowning.

"Yes." She hesitated only momentarily. "My father tried to drown me at the lake when I was eight. I see him grab me and hold me underwater. That's what it feels like in the cemetery."

"Is there anything you want to say to him?"

Again I prompted Marie with the active verb; however, as with Chris, she had the other character do all the talking. "He's there angry. He says I never said good-bye to *him*. That's true; two weeks before he died, we had a terrible fight. He beat me so bad, my dress was ripped off. I wasn't speaking to him. Then one day he said he wanted to talk to me. I didn't call him back. The next day he had a heart attack."

"If you want to see what he might say now, you can try and listen."

"He says the same thing as always, 'I'm sorry.' " Her voice took on a touch of bitterness as she imitated him. " 'I was drunk. Give me another chance'—just the same old thing. Then Chris's there, saying, 'Leave her alone, I took your demons.' She means the drink and violence. 'They are buried with me now. Marie won't take them.' " There was a long pause. "He's really gone now. Chris always protected me, but she says Daddy is buried and I'm strong enough to protect myself now."

"Is there anything else you want to do in that scene?"

"No."

"Then let the graveyard fade from your mind's eye. As I count from ten to one backwards, you will begin to wake up. . . ."

When she opened her eyes, Marie immediately smiled. "It was great to see the house looking different. . . . Like seeing the future."

"Do you think you'll fix it that way?"

"Probably. It looked right."

"What did that 'Madame Curie' mean?" I asked her.

"Nobody's used that in years. That's what Chris and lots of the kids at school called me back in seventh or eighth grade when science was my favorite subject."

"Do you have any idea why that would come up now?"

"Well, I had considered this lab technician training program. The state unemployment office runs it along with three biotech companies. If you do well in it, you get a job at one of them. Maybe I should do that after all, instead of joining the army."

I was pleased with Marie's positive insights, but I also wanted to deal with the darker material that had arisen. "Your father tried to drown you?" I did not ask again why she had said her life included no other traumas. By now it was obvious that she minimized the family's problems— both to outsiders like me and to herself.

"Well, yes." She was more reticent already now that she was out of trance. "At least I thought I was going to drown. He finally let me up."

I did not want to challenge her defenses further by inquiring about that strange, indirect phrase: "beat me up so bad my dress was ripped off." The answer to one puzzle with Marie tended to raise another, we were building quite a list of topics we were not going to be able to deal with if closure was to come in this session.

"You have so many things going on in your life. Are you sure you don't want to come back a few more times to talk about them?"

"No, I already feel like I can begin to leave Chris's death behind me and get on with my life."

Not wanting to undercut her momentum, I started bidding Marie good-bye. I told her she was welcome to call if she had any more questions. "Thank you," she said as she exited. "I remembered what I came for and seeing Chris today in the hypnosis was really wonderful."

Nancy, as the middle-class daughter of a physician, had gravitated toward psychotherapy. In Marie's subculture, one usually goes to a priest to discuss depression or other troubles, even something like Marie's odd perceptions of gunshots and ghosts. It took the reputation of hypnosis to lure her outside her usual channels. Therapists are in some sense the new priests of the agnostic temples of Western science and medicine. Hypnosis probably fits into this role the best of all Western therapies.

Aside from the poltergeistlike phenomena in my office and Marie's house, her sister Chris was a "noisy ghost" in other senses. Although Marie did not want her too vigorously exorcised, the hypnosis had quieted her down.

6
Saint Joan

"Terese Lafolette, twenty-five-year-old female," the inpatient consult request read. "Please evaluate whether hypnosis would be useful for her intrusive traumatic flashbacks. See on unit, level-two suicide precautions." I was pleased to receive a request which recognized that hypnosis can modulate an overactive memory. Nonhypnotists often stereotype hypnotherapy as useful only for increasing recall.

The inpatient unit I entered to see Terese was a place of odd contrasts. A key-bearing attendant admitted me through a heavy metal door into a dark hallway, where two disheveled patients ignored me as I passed—one motionless, the other rocking and moaning. Yet as I approached the dayroom, I could have been in a college dorm: well-groomed women sat on the flowered sofa watching a *Three's Company* rerun, laughing and making jokes about their own roommates.

I entered the circular glass nurses' station adjoining the dayroom. "I have a consult to see Terese Lafolette," I told the white-uniformed nurse preparing the afternoon medications. "I'd like to look at her chart before I interview her."

The nurse handed me a gray binder overflowing with photocopied records from other hospitals as well as pages logging the current stay. She returned to counting brightly colored pills into paper demitasse cups. Perching on the edge of the counter, I began reading the handwritten page that preceded the usual intake form.

"I promise not to attempt to harm myself. If I feel that I am going to do so, I will tell my doctor or nursing staff immediately. Sincerely, Terese." A legion of other signatures followed—neat and messy, childish and adult, masculine and feminine. All were bland names: Patti, Kenny, Joseph, Veronica . . . until the final signature in flourishing calligraphic script: Joan d'Arc.

The three diagnoses on the following intake page were hardly a surprise: depressive episode with suicidal features, post-traumatic stress disorder, and multiple personality.

I skimmed the intake summary:

Twenty-five-year-old college-educated female . . . severe traumas since early childhood, including physical and sexual abuse by patient's father, who is a

high-level official in the State Department. . . .
strangulation attempt by her paternal uncle. . . .
mother failed to protect . . . has younger brother,
who was also abused. Brother lives in Boston, good
relationship with patient. . . .

Two alters speak only French, one Russian, one
writes in Hebrew, and an autistic one doesn't speak.
There are three Greek "Muses."

I was beginning to think that not every one of Terese's
alters besides the saint of the arc was so bland—multina-
tional personalities are not common.

One alter seems to represent the child who was
nearly murdered by the uncle.

The patient has intermittent success as a concert pianist, and is also reputed to have some talent
as an artist and a poet. . . . She has not performed
since the first of three recent hospitalizations. . . .
Current roommates have asked her to find another
apartment because of last suicide attempt.

"Could you point Terese out to me?" I asked the nurse
as I returned the chart to a bookshelf full of its clones.
"And is there a quiet place free for me to interview her?"

"She doesn't have a regular room yet. She's in the
seclusion room because of suicide attempts and other disturbances. You'll need to talk to her in there so we can
keep doing ten-minute suicide checks." She laid down the
pills, locked the nurses' station, and led me briskly down
the hall. I knew better than to argue with the institutional
logic that required the unit's staff taking time to ascertain

that a patient was not committing suicide in full view of an outpatient staff member of the same hospital.

"That's Terese," the nurse said, pointing through the high, square window of a tiny room. Opening the unlocked door, she called in, "Someone's here to see you." Without waiting for an answer, she pivoted and disappeared down the hall. Hesitantly, I entered the room.

Terese was a thin, androgynous young woman with large, waiflike eyes and short, brown hair. She wore a shapeless black turtleneck sweater and baggy jeans. I've seen multiple personalities of all descriptions: some with long hair or lots of makeup. About 10 percent of them are men. However, since Dolores, all the multiples I'd seen had been young women of small stature with the same childlike features, short tousled dark hair, and genderless clothing. This appearance seemed to constitute a compromise between male and female personalities. Therefore, Terese looked oddly familiar, reminding me of several previous patients. She huddled on a mattress in the middle of the floor. The room's walls were padded and covered in white vinyl—as if wallpapered with giant exercise mats. The only other furnishings were two chairs upholstered in white leatherette which almost matched the walls. The "seclusion" room served many purposes and could be locked for violent patients.

Terese stared down at the mattress, not appearing to notice me as I closed the door and stood in the bit of unoccupied floor space. "Terese?" I ventured, although I knew the odds were not high that this was what she called herself at the moment. She was slow to turn her face toward me, but then she did become alert and regarded me with polite interest.

"I'm Dr. Barrett. Your physician asked me to come talk to you to decide if hypnosis might be of any help with the problems you're having."

"Oh yes—she told me!" Terese's face and frame were fully animated now. "Please have a seat." Gesturing to one of the chairs, she scrambled up to sit in the other. She looked completely the hospitable college freshman welcoming me to her dorm room. Terese had moved from resembling the worst-functioning patients on the unit to the best in the space of a minute.

"I've looked at your written records a bit, but I'd like to hear things in your own words. Can you tell me why you're in the hospital now?"

"I'm a multiple and a trauma survivor. I guess you read that. Besides me—I'm the 'host personality'—there are ten alters that I know about. Only six ever have full executive control, and only three are out much." This language was the opposite of the way Dolores and her family had described puzzling events. Terese used more jargon of the multiple personality field than did I or most mental health professionals. 'Host' is the term therapists might use among themselves to refer to the dominant personality, but it sounded ironic as a way to perceive oneself.

"I only realized that my blackouts were related to my dissociation two years ago, and I've had more trouble controlling it lately," Terese told me. "My last therapist said that's because I lost the structure of college. January was a month when many traumatic things happened, so it gets worse this time of year." I didn't ask specifics, although I was curious whether she remembered these things directly or whether she just knew her alters were having difficult flashbacks. Some multiples in therapy begin to have many of the same memories across personalities before they integrate. For others, the host personality learns of events from the past only when he or she hears a "voice" describing them.

A male attendant peered through the small window. Terese bugged her eyes out in an exaggerated imitation of him. I stifled a laugh, sensing her contempt for the unit's regimen; I did not want to be seen as endorsing her attitude.

"Why are you in the seclusion room?" I asked. I didn't know what the nurse had meant by "other disturbances."

"Just for being a multiple, I guess. I don't think they understand much about ego state psychology." Again she spoke in the jargon of the field more than most professionals.

"Because of what about being a multiple?" I persisted.

"Well, my child alters come out. Benji hides under the table and can't talk, and Patti only knows French when she's frightened. The nurses just say, 'Speak English,' loudly, over and over. Patti can't. They said dayroom rules include no baby talk, no foreign languages unless you *are* foreign, no rocking or head banging. Well, like, *hello*?" Terese intoned sarcastically. "If I could do that, I probably wouldn't have come into a mental hospital, would I? And never mind that there's two schizophrenics in there. One's talking to his hallucinations—they're okay, my alters aren't. The other one's speaking some kind of Martian word salad—that's fine, just not French."

Terese's tone softened. "I don't care, I like it in seclusion. There's a nurse on the night shift who comes in and speaks French. She even says 'Patti.' That's another thing they say you can't do." I shared some of Terese's views of what was unproductive about trying to suppress dissociation during a hospitalization. Another diagnostic group, borderline personalities—whose conditions are also related to childhood trauma—are often perceived by both inpatient staff and outside therapists as engaging in annoying manipulation and attention seeking. Inpatient staff typically view multiple personalities this way, while their outside therapists are sympathetic. I could already see a potential for such a split with Terese.

"Your chart mentioned suicidality and they have you on suicide watch, not foreign language watch." Terese laughed, but I didn't want to make too light of it, so I added in a more serious tone, "Are you suicidal?"

"Well, not me, host-Terese, but yes, I have suicidal alters. I switch to Joan who wants to die. That's the reason for all four of my hospitalizations. I used to just take pills or cut and not remember. Now I know it's Joan who does that." She sounded concerned in the way one might speak about a depressed friend.

"And the consult mentioned you have flashbacks?"

"Yes, Patti sees my father. Recently, it's him standing with a skillet, cooking meat and she thinks it's human flesh—I think he told her that. That's when she panics and Joan comes out and wants to be a martyr."

"Your alter is Joan of Arc, the saint?"

"First she was just plain Joan. Then we lived in France when I was five to nine 'cause my father was stationed at the embassy there. Joan decided she was French 'cause she learned the language and Catholic 'cause she felt safe in the cathedrals. Just before we left France, we saw the film *The Passion of Joan of Arc*. When Joan watched it, she decided that it was about her. She's been a saint and a martyr ever since."

Indeed, an alter can either begin as an internalization of an actual individual and diverge in development or begin as an abstraction and adopt a real individual's traits. At the trial of the Hillside Strangler, psychologist Martin Orne argued that the "Steve" personality who admitted to the murders must be fake because he claimed to have existed from childhood yet used the last name of someone he had met recently. Other psychologists such as John Watson, who were more experienced in working with multiples, testified that this was not inconsistent with multiple personalities. I don't know if the Strangler was a multiple or an impostor—that's still one of the great debates in hypnosis circles—but Orne's argument is not a basis on which to rule out multiplicity.

Terese widened her eyes in a sarcastic stare at a point behind me. I knew, without even glancing at the door, that the attendant was doing his check again. As my time on the unit was running short, I shifted to talking about how hypnosis might be able to help. I offered my standard explanation of dissociation as already much like an informal trance. I described how hypnosis could harness the ability to create imagery to replace vivid imaginings of past horrors with soothing scenes. I explained that it would take several sessions to learn such techniques and make some tapes with which she could practice on her own. Terese asked the same questions about hypnosis that an academically interested college student might, rather than nervous ones about being the subject of it. She was eager to try. "Oh yes, Dr. Hardy recommended it, and you. She's the only one around here who seems to know anything about MPD." I agreed to see Terese on my next available hour, which was the Friday four days hence. By the time the attendant made his next check, I was ready to ask him to let me off the unit.

On Friday, Terese was in the hall as the attendant admitted me. "I already checked with the nurses' station. They said we can use interview room three," she announced brightly. With another patient, I might have confirmed this or at least touched base with the staff. However, Terese seemed like someone who would be both accurate in her information and insulted if I asked staff to corroborate the details she'd just given me.

I headed for the designated room. As soon as we were inside, she began an animated monologue. "I got out of seclusion on Wednesday morning. I have a roommate, Carli. She's a multiple too. She's great! Two of her alters are deaf and use sign language. She's teaching sign to Benji 'cause he can't speak. My alter Joseph is teaching Hebrew to one of her alters who's Jewish but never went to Hebrew school . . ." My head spun as I tried to keep straight these interactions. The tragic aspects of multiple personality are usually emphasized, but it has a fanciful side. After all, it begins with creative kids making up a world in which to escape trauma. Another multiple I'd seen on the same unit, in addition to her own personalities, was convinced that the stuffed teddy bear she'd had since childhood changed personalities from Teddy to Grizzly. I listened to Terese's tale about Carli trying to convince the inpatient staff that a deaf alter shouldn't be required to answer spoken questions. "They're threatening her with seclusion, too, 'cause she's a multiple," she added conspiratorially.

I squelched the impulse to ask, "It wouldn't be that she's also in here for serious suicidality, would it?" I preferred to shift the focus away from either encouraging or disagreeing with Terese's assessment of the unit.

"Are you ready for hypnosis?" I asked. She nodded, suddenly the model of attentiveness.

"Today I want to try the first exercise to help you feel better when you're upset. It will be mainly for you, Terese, but if any of your alters want to follow along, or just listen to it, that's okay. Afterwards, we'll decide whether this one's best for them. Some of them might prefer a kind of relaxation that's more for children." Just as adult multiples often keep stuffed toys and watch Disney movies, therapy techniques developed for real children can help with anxious child alters. Critics sometimes oppose this as reinforcing childishness. I don't agree; these people did not have a normal childhood. A period of such indulgences usually helps to grow past needing them.

"Just close your eyes and begin to relax. Let your breathing become slow and deep." I talked Terese through a standard induction until she appeared to be in a trance. Then I began the specific suggestions.

"You can picture in your mind's eye a safe place, somewhere that you find beautiful, serene, and calming. Let the safe place take shape as you look around and note its details. . . . Are you outdoors in nature, or is your safe place inside? Is the lighting bright or dim? You can look around at everything there. . . . Are there beautiful objects or colors that contribute to the sense of calm and happiness? Are you alone in your safe place, or is there a trusted

person—or maybe even a nice animal—there with you?
. . . Is the sense of safety associated with warmth or cool-
ness? Do you hear any special soothing sounds? Are there
pleasant smells? If you want, you can reach out and touch
objects to feel their textures." I elaborated more potential
embellishments. "Once you have noted all the details of
your safe place, you can just relax there, drawing strength
and nurturance from your surroundings. I am going to be
silent for a little while as you just rest in your safe place."

I waited about three minutes while a slight smile
played over Terese's face, then resumed. "Now in a moment, when you're ready, I want you to begin to let the
image of your safe place fade from your mind's eye. You
can keep the sense of safety and relaxation and bring that
with you. In the future, if you like, you will be able to find
your way back to it easily and surely. But for now, let the
image fade away." I counted her awake.

"What was that like?" I asked.

"I loved it. I went to a clearing in the woods," she told
me. "The trees grow so dense around it that you can only
get in at one break between two oaks. Branches grow
over it so that they almost make a roof. Instead of sky, you
see a high ceiling of green leaves with sunlight filtering
through them like an abstract stained-glass window.
There's a pond and moss and lots of little wildflowers—
pink and yellow buttercups. I sat on the moss and looked
up and just sort of meditated. It was beautiful."

"Did any of your other personalities do this with you?"

"They didn't do the hypnosis, but they listened to see
if I was okay."

"Were you nervous about me or the hypnosis?"

"I wasn't, but some of my alters were."

"Me or the hypnosis?"

"Oh, both. Some of them don't trust anybody or anything at first. But they didn't find anything wrong with it. Some of them might even do it next time." I've treated multiples who said they wouldn't even close their eyes in my presence. After one or two sessions of eyes-open relaxation, they usually become comfortable and shut them without active persuading.

"If this isn't the right relaxation for them, like I said, we could talk about some techniques for children."

"No, they liked this."

"They can have different safe places during the same suggestions," I added. "Next time, we'll see if there are any changes that would make this exercise better, and then we'll tape it. Meanwhile, over the weekend, you can practice remembering the safe place if you need to distract yourself from other images." I made another appointment with her for Monday afternoon. In learning traumatic-stress reduction techniques, short but frequent visits are more useful than the typical one-hour-per-week psychotherapy.

"Good-bye," I said as we exited the interview room. "I'll see you Monday."

"Good-bye," Terese replied. I walked a few more steps and heard a tiny, childlike voice add, "Au revoir."

"Au revoir," I managed, with great surprise and poor pronunciation. I wanted to acknowledge the new speaker but didn't think it was the time to get into a conversation with—Patti? Joan? They were the two alters who I knew spoke French.

When I returned to the unit for our third session, Terese presented me with a large sheet of paper. She held it up for inspection—a watercolor, obviously done quickly but with deft, evocative strokes. An emerald green was applied with a spongelike pattern to denote the forest encircling a clear space with the solid blue of the pond in the center. Simple black lines formed branches with lime green leaves overhead; pink and yellow dabs of abstract flowers dotted the foreground. "Thinking of this place made me feel better all weekend, except when Patti got frightened imagining my father. Then I couldn't get any control over what we were thinking about. In art group on Sunday, they wanted us to do a watercolor. I painted the clearing and hung it over my bed. That made the hospital room seem more like it was mine." Therapists often ask patients to draw or paint images from dreams or hypnosis to bring them into the real world. Terese hit upon this technique without my suggesting it.

She continued with an account of her weekend. "I can't practice 'cause there's no piano here. I'm so afraid of losing my ability to play. But my brother visited. That was nice, except I always feel guilty about him. I'm the older sister, but he ends up taking care of me—worrying about my suicide attempts, helping me out financially, everything. Also, I did terrible things to him when he was little." She grimaced and shifted in her chair. "I don't want to talk about that."

"The nurses have been threatening to separate Carli and I, but they haven't yet. They say we're a bad influence on each other, so we're trying not to let them see us using sign language or speaking Hebrew or French. Carli's boyfriend was here and I met him. He'd brought Herman, her Vietnamese potbellied pig. They wouldn't let Herman on the unit, and they wouldn't let Carli go down to the parking lot even for a minute." Terese's voice was full of indignation. "Carli ended up having a fight with her boyfriend as well as the nurses when he tried to tell her she didn't really need to see Herman. She doesn't think he takes good care of Herman. He's supposed to give him a bubble bath every two days and he doesn't. She thinks he doesn't like the pig 'cause he's jealous. She lets Herman sleep in her bed. Well . . . I can see how that might bother her boyfriend," she allowed—the only chink in the fortress of her together-with-Carli-against-the-world perspective.

"Speaking of meeting people," I shifted, "who said 'good-bye' to me in French last time?"

"That was Patti. She'd been listening and decided you were nice."

"Maybe she'll do hypnosis with us today. I'm going to make a tape for you to listen to between sessions. There are two options we could try today. I could talk very generally like I did last time, so that each alter might find a different safe place, or I could describe the scene in the woods since you said everyone liked that."

"Do the clearing; we've all been thinking about it." Multiple personality patients who are not aware of their disorder say "I" meaning whichever alter is talking at the time. Ones with good communication among personalities who are moving toward integration often say "we," speaking for all the personalities. Terese alternated between these pronouns, I noticed.

"Okay. This time Patti and Joan and whoever else wants to learn to feel safe can do hypnosis. Maybe you'll be there together, or maybe each personality will see herself or himself alone in the clearing, whichever you prefer." A therapist also has a delicate task in choosing how to refer to multiple personality alters. I don't want to introduce more distance than they perceive among parts of the self. At times, it is even necessary to emphatically remind them that they are one person with shared responsibility for their actions. On the other hand, it's important to use language that acknowledges their subjective sense of separate identities.

After an induction, I repeated some of the general suggestions I'd given in the last session about finding a setting that was safe and relaxing. This time I combined them with details of Terese's particular safe place. Now in the place of the alternatives—"you could be outdoors or inside"—I described the details of the clearing. Instead of "just feeling protected by the place," it was being protected "by the thick oaks encircling you." Noticing the lighting became "Notice how peaceful the soft light filtering through the leaves above you is." The soothing colors were embodied by "the pink and yellow of the buttercups." "If you like, you can reach out and touch the velvety moss or cool water" replaced just "feel textures." Occasionally, I glanced at the watercolor on the desk to get a better sense of the space I was talking Terese into.

Finally I was quiet as I gave her time to simply enjoy being there. Different demeanors—childlike, serious, serene—played across her face, as if each of the personalities sat there for a moment. These were gradual transitions, not the dramatic switches multiples make when awake. After a few minutes, I brought her out of the trance by counting backwards and turned off the tape recorder.

"That was great," Terese announced. "I went to the same place and liked it even more."

"Were any of your other personalities with you?"

"Yes, but they all did different things there. Patti curled up in the hollow of a big tree, where it was dark and secure because no one could see her. Kenny thought it was a safe place to play because there was no one there to yell at him. He picked grubs from under the moss and climbed way up in a tree out of sight. He found some spotted beetles and was playing with them.

"Joan rode up on a white horse. She tied it outside the clearing before she entered. She ignored the beauty—she's real ascetic, you know"—this apparently referred to my knowledge of the historic figure. "She waded into the pond and asked it if it would take her to God—she wanted to drown. But it's a safe pond that you can't drown in. Instead, she floated on her back with her arms out like in a crucifixion. The water was holy water that heals. It took away all the pain. She heard you talking about being at peace and thought it was the voice of God. She's listening to me now and arguing." Terese paused and then appeared to respond to Joan's queries. "That's our *therapist*." She looked back at me. "Joan doesn't believe me; she still has you confused with God."

Freud wrote about "transference" as the tendency to see a therapist as a parent or other primitive authority figure. My elevation to supreme being was far and away the most naked transference I'd ever heard. "Countertransference" is Freud's term for the illogical feelings with which therapists respond to their patients. That covered the rush of dismay and affection that washed over me. When I knew someone attached such profound significance to whatever I said, any simple statement sounded trite. I handed Terese the tape and managed, "Just listen to this at least once a day to practice relaxation and more if there are times you feel especially unsafe. Is it okay to meet the same time on Friday?"

"Sure." Terese rose and collected her watercolor. As we left the interview room, we passed another young woman with short, dark hair. "Carli!" Terese exclaimed. "Meet Dr. Barrett." Carli gave me a slight smile and said, "I've heard really good things about you." She had those same androgynous, childlike features, with a more reserved and serious demeanor. As Terese began to recount her new experiences to Carli, I excused myself to enter the nurses' station and write a progress note in Terese's chart. While I was bent over the vinyl folder, Dr. Elizabeth Hardy entered. "Hi, thanks for referring Terese," I told her. "She seems to be quite hypnotizable."

"Yes, I know she's enthusiastic about it. The team was wondering if you have time in your outpatient schedule to see her. We're hoping to discharge Terese in a week or so, and we want to give her an outpatient referral. She'll be in a day treatment program six hours a day at first, but it would be good for her to have something more psychodynamic. Her case worker at day treatment will mostly be checking that she's eating regularly, sleeping okay, taking her meds, and not planning to overdose. You could see her until you've done everything that's useful with hypnosis and then refer her to someone for general therapy. Or you could keep seeing her for that, too."

"You're not going to follow her yourself?"

"No, I'd like to. She's so interesting, and I've worked a fair bit with dissociative disorders. But right now I'm assigned full-time to inpatient duties."

"Well, yes, certainly. Tell her I'm available if she wants to continue after she's discharged."

Any topic of special importance to a patient interests me by what it may reveal about his or her beliefs and fantasies. I've familiarized myself with obscure artists, songwriters, and even my patients' favorite stand-up comics to see what distinctive aspects of the world they portray. Two decades ago, I watched TV's *The Incredible Hulk* to get a feel for the fear and desire for unleashed anger that prompted a very inhibited ten-year-old patient's obsession with the show. I'm a film buff and even write a movie review column for the magazine *DreamTime*. However, silent films are not my genre, so I hadn't seen the 1928 *Passion of Joan of Arc*.

Wednesday, I was done with work early and dropped by my local video store. In my Harvard Square neighborhood, obscure oldies are easy to find. I watched *Passion* that night. It is set on the last day of Joan's trial. We do not see her in good times leading her troops. We see only the stark black-and-white images of Joan, played by the lovely but androgynous Maria Falconetti, clad in a man's tunic, leggings, and boots shackled before her gloating sadistic male inquisitors. The grim terror of the verbal and physical tortures she endures are all the more awful because the viewer knows the inevitable conclusion. Throughout the silent film, Joan's huge sad eyes show at first suffering, then otherworldly remove as she goes to her fiery death.

According to the video's cover, Falconetti never acted again, saying that she had poured everything of herself into that one role. This was the performance from which Terese's alter drew inspiration and her very identity.

"They're discharging me!" Terese announced happily when I arrived Friday. "They said you'd be my outpatient therapist. I'm set to leave Monday morning after Dr. Hardy makes her rounds. That means I won't be here for our Monday appointment time. I guess I could come over to the outpatient building later, but I'd rather not. There's something depressing about getting out of the hospital and coming back on the same day. Of course, if they don't let Carli out too, I'll be coming back to visit her. But I think she'll be discharged next week, too." Terese continued her breathless monologue. "If it's okay with you, I'd rather wait until Friday. You *are* going to be my outpatient therapist, aren't you?"

"Yes, I am. I suppose we could wait a week. After today's session, you'll have two tapes to be listening to. They told me you'd be in day treatment. Where will you be living?" I remembered her previous roommates had ordered her out.

"I don't have a place yet, but I have appointments to look at three places this weekend. If none of them work out, I'm eligible to stay at the women's shelter for up to two weeks. That's last choice 'cause I couldn't have my piano there."

"Why don't you call Tuesday or Wednesday just to leave me your new number and let me know you're okay?"

"Sure, even the shelter has a phone number I could be reached at."

"How was the weekend?"

"Mostly good. Carli taught Benji more words in sign. And last night she showed me a new trick. Sometimes when I 'switch,' I have trouble getting back. Carli said two personalities could just join hands and swing around a hundred and eighty degrees. Then the one who was out is back in—and vice versa. I tried it when Patti was out and wanted back in. It works and it's kind of fun, too." Apparently, Terese and Carli shared the strange logic of this imagery system.

It reminded me of an anorexic patient of mine several years before who was slowly putting weight back on her skeletal frame when she began to complain about her stomach bulging. No matter how staunchly the staff and I reassured her that her stomach was still concave, she couldn't be calmed. However, another recovered anorexic patient assured her that weight always goes to the stomach first. The other patient explained that one had to endure a potbelly for a few weeks and then the weight would spread out through the arms and legs. I don't think this had any basis in physical reality, but it was extremely comforting to my patient, who proceeded to experience her continued weight gain in exactly this way. Patients with the same diagnoses can be uniquely helpful to each other through their shared perspective. However, they also have the unique potential to exacerbate each other's problems. The latter is what tempted the inpatient staff to separate Terese and Carli.

"I listened to the tape every day," Terese continued. "That worked well except Patti had a bad time on Tuesday. She saw my dad like he was in the corner of the room cooking meat. I couldn't get back out to put the tape on. Carli wasn't there 'cause they made her sleep in the seclusion room. She'd tried to cut herself with a plastic knife. It was only a scratch." I was getting the picture that Carli—for all her sound advice and preference to play an older sister role to Terese's dependent one—was at least as unable to help herself.

"You mentioned the scene with the meat before. Is it a memory or what?"

"I'm not completely sure. Patti was always the one to deal with my father's scary behavior except the sexual stuff—that was Veronica. Patti remembers that she came into the kitchen and asked what he was doing. He said he was cooking a little girl who'd made him mad. He said it real mean, not like he was joking. Patti thinks he was really cooking a person, but I guess it was just beef and he said that. Anyway, she never ate meat again and she's afraid of being cooked. That's what she told our last therapist about the memory. The image Patti keeps seeing isn't that involved—there's no soundtrack. She just sees my father standing there cooking and feels terrified. She used to see him like that at our apartment. Then, when Patti couldn't stand it any longer, Joan would come out and want to kill herself and become a martyr."

"I've been wondering about that," I said. "You can't become a martyr by killing yourself. You only become a martyr when someone else kills you. The Catholic church teaches that suicide is the worst sin because it's the only one you have no chance to repent afterward. They certainly don't make you a saint for it. People who are so unhappy that they want to die are supposed to pray for help in getting past that feeling." I knew I ran a risk of making Joan feel more guilty. However, as I mentioned in Chapter 5, Catholicism is one of the strong protective factors against suicide and I wanted to invoke this.

"Yeah, I guess I've heard that. Joan got her education from films and storybooks about the saints."

Terese looked upward again as she had last time. "Joan says I'm patronizing her, but she's going to check on that thing about suicide."

Obviously my opinion was no longer confused with the word of God. I moved on. "The exercise we're going to do today will help with the flashbacks.

"Close your eyes and let yourself begin to relax. . . ." I talked Terese into a trance, then focused my suggestions on her flashbacks. "Think of any bad images that disturb you, ones you'd like to lock away. You can look around you and find something that you could shut them in. Notice if it is a giant box or trunk. Maybe it's a vault or a safe with a massive door, possibly a deep hole in the earth. At first, as I mention these containers, you may see images of several of them. Gradually you will settle on one that will be best for holding your disturbing images.

"Once you see that container clearly, you can take an image that's bothering you and put it inside. Throw it in there or stuff it in, or have a helper do that for you if you don't want to touch it. Now take the next bad image and throw it in too. Each one stays there securely while you keep adding to the pile, until every bad image is in the container." I paused to give her time to complete this task. "When everything that you want to get rid of is inside, you can close or seal it any way you like. You can lock it, shut and bar a huge door, put chains around your container, or bury it.

"Next," I continued, "send the container far away from you, however you like. You can drop it into the ocean, shoot it into space, or just walk away, leaving it far, far behind. You know that everything you don't want to see now is safely locked away in this container that represents the past. If you ever need or want to think about it, you can retrieve any item to examine it. But for now, it's locked away where it won't bother you. You know these things are not in the present but far away—they belong to the past. In the future, you'll be able to use this imagery with anything from the past that's bothering you if it's not the time to think about it." I counted her back to waking.

"Did you lock everything away?"

"Terese and Patti and Kenny did. Each one locked theirs in a different place. Patti saw my dad with the knife and the meat in the skillet. She pictured him being stuffed into a huge glass flask. She put a stopper in it and floated the flask away out to sea.

"Terese saw something similar about herself being burned in a skillet as her soul leaves her body. She made this into an oil painting, and she saw robed monks carrying the picture into a vault like the one under the Vatican. They locked the vault and sprinkled holy water all around the door so no evil could get out." I'd heard bizarre fictional accounts of what was supposed to be in the Vatican's vaults: plundered treasure, dissenting gospels, and the (unascended) mummy of Jesus—I guess Joan's version was no odder.

"Kenny saw a huge medieval wooden trunk with a hinged lid. He and his band of men—kind of like Robin

Hood's—threw images of my uncle into it. When everything was in, gnomes and trolls came and eased the heavy
lid down. They threw a big iron bolt through it. Then
more trolls came with chains and wrapped them all
around the trunk and padlocked it. They dragged the
trunk onto an old cart with wooden wheels. There were
two thick ropes in front of the cart and they pulled it
away. They took it over a drawbridge to a castle with a
dungeon. After the cart was across, they raised the drawbridge so that nothing could escape."

"All this while I was talking?"

"Yes, everyone did their locking away at the same
time." Her parallel imagery was remarkable. I'm not sure I
could have produced the trolls' cart alone, much less
while simultaneously thinking up the Vatican and a sealed
flask under the ocean.

I handed Terese the tape of this exercise and suggested she could listen to it if she continued to be both-
ered by intrusive flashbacks. I bid her good-bye, aware
that the next time I saw her it would be as an outpatient.

"Hello?" I answered my phone when it rang between patients' appointments the following Tuesday.

"Is this Dr. Barrett?" There were barking noises in the
background. I almost didn't recognize the distant and re-
spectful voice. I was accustomed to the friendly, informal
one.

"Oh, hi Terese. How are you doing?" The barks continued.

"Pretty good. I'm glad to be out. I just finished my second day at the treatment center."

"Do you have a place yet?"

"I'm staying with Carli. She got out yesterday morning, too. She's already back at work. She doesn't have to go to day treatment . . . *Ahhhhh* . . . no, ouch!" The barking had become fiercer and alternated with snarls.

"Are you all right? Is that dog after you?"

"It's not a dog. Everything's okay now. I'm standing on the kitchen table. I was only on a chair before and he could almost get me. Let me give you this number." She read the seven digits over more snarling. "I'll be here until Friday. I'm scheduled to look at two apartments Thursday. I'm sure I'll take one."

"What do you mean, 'It's not a dog?' " I demanded, barely having processed the phone number.

"That's Herman," Terese replied. It took me a moment to place the name.

"The *pig?*" I asked incredulously. I realized I'd never heard a Vietnamese miniature potbellied pig, at least not an angry one. My only encounters with the species were at the Harvard research lab where human psychology shared space with psychopharmaceutical research. The breed is popular for drug testing because their diet and metabolism are close to those of humans. Occasionally as I walked someone down the hall, a pharmacologist would appear with several hundred pounds' worth of the misnamed "miniatures" in a harness and leash. Such constitutionals did not aid in recruiting human subjects, although their porcine counterparts waddled by with no more than a friendly snuffle. After all, the Harvard pigs' whole raison d'être was to absorb large quantities of new tranquilizers.

"Yeah. Herman hates me," Terese continued. "He tries to bite me whenever I come in the kitchen. I'm not supposed to shut him up here, but I do when Carli's gone. At first I was thinking of living with her permanently because her boyfriend moved out after a fight about Herman. But I can't." The snarling and barking continued unabated.

"Are you sure you're okay?" At least her suicidality and post-traumatic stress disorder seemed under control.

"Yeah. I can climb from the table to the counter and out the door without him reaching me. Kenny actually thinks it's kind of fun. Herman behaves when Carli's here. She'll be home soon. Don't worry," she said like a kid to an overanxious mom. "I'm using the tapes." I reflected that perhaps Terese needed real trolls to deal with Herman. Trauma survivors often gravitate toward chaotic environments and accept all manner of nastiness as a given. Terese's current situation was both comical and under control, but the same tendencies can be deadly in other trauma survivors.

By our Friday session, Terese had made a deposit on an apartment with money borrowed from her brother. She would be moving in the next day. Her immediate complaints had shifted from Herman to her withdrawal from medication. The outpatient psychopharmacology clinic had refused to continue prescribing for her because she had repeatedly broken her contracts not to overdose. The type of written contract I'd found in the front of her inpatient chart was standard for suicidal patients. It works well for patients for whom the concept of a promise to someone else inhibits suicide attempts. For others, such as Terese, though, the contract is irrelevant when they are in acute distress. No one felt her medication was essential or arrangements would have been made for her day treatment center to hand pills out one at a time.

Perhaps it's not surprising that multiple personalities often get put on multiple medications; antianxiety drugs get prescribed when one personality is anxious, antidepressants for another, Ritalin when only one personality has attention problems, even Thorazine when the host describes hearing voices commanding her to do things. Schizophrenia has long been described as including symptoms called the positive signs: auditory hallucinations, visual hallucinations, delusions of being controlled, and a sense of others "inserting" thoughts into one's head. Recent research finds that these are actually more common in patients with multiple personality disorder than in schizophrenics. This leads to much confusion among diagnosing physicians, even though the same research finds that MPD's display none of the negative signs of schizophrenia—flat emotion, poor comprehension of social norms, detachment from others, concrete thinking, and confused reasoning.

I've seen multiples improve when removed from a long list of medications. The only drug giving Terese problems since its discontinuance was the sleeping pill she had been taking. Physiological withdrawal was exacerbating her previous insomnia and she was having nightmares once asleep. Terese wondered whether hypnosis might help.

Even mildly hypnotizable insomniacs benefit from the physical relaxation of hypnosis and the direction of attention away from troubling thoughts. Terese, being highly hypnotizable, might have been able to override the drug withdrawal the same way one can control the perception of pain, the flow of blood, or histamine release in response to poison ivy as I mentioned in Chapter 4. Trauma patients' insomnia is also usually related to their PTSD. Multiple personalities often have one or more "protector" alters who rescue or at least comfort them. I wondered whether Terese did. I asked her if any of her personalities were ever helpful with anything like her sleep problem. She said the Three Muses were there to "watch or protect." I suggested we call on them as part of the hypnotic exercise and she agreed. I did a brief induction.

"See yourself getting ready for bed," I told her. "You're switching off the overhead light, pulling back your covers, and getting into bed. You turn off the lamp beside the bed and snuggle down under the blankets. Now ask the Muses to come. Think about what they could do or say to help you feel safe. Maybe they'll tell you something reassuring. Maybe they'll give you some kind of present that makes you feel safe. Maybe there's some ritual you know. They could sing you a song. Just watch and see what they do. It will be just right to relax you and make you feel safe."

"They're forming a circle around me," Terese narrated, "clasping their hands so I'm completely enclosed. At first they sway to the left and then to the right, like it's a dance. Then they stand still like statues—well, more like angels, protecting me."

"You can see yourself beginning to drift off to sleep, feeling very safe with them standing guard. . . . Maybe when they finish this ritual, they will want to lie down and go to sleep."

"No," Terese replied emphatically. "They are going to stay around me all night."

"They don't want to rest, too?"

"No," she said, as if explaining to a schoolchild. "The Muses are not mortal. They do not need to sleep." Terese seemed much more certain of her Greek mythology than she had been of her Catholic theology. "Okay." Not only were the Muses not mortal, they were not real. I supposed they did not necessarily need to sleep. It seemed wisest to trust Terese's intuitive feel for this. I made her a tape of the ritual of the Muses encircling her while she slept and sent her home with it.

People with MPD often experience a variety of odd sleep phenomena. Multiples may describe one personality "sleeping" while another is awake and, unlike Terese's Muses, moving around in the body. Others have alters who are awake but cannot move until the host awakens— the Muses seemed to function this way. One patient I saw only "switched" during sleep; other personalities had to wait for the host to doze off before they could assume control. Some multiples simply have personalities who all sleep at the same time.

I did a study of dreams in MPD, which is described in more detail in my book *Trauma and Dreams.* I found several ways patients' dreams interacted with this disorder. Before realizing they were multiples, many patients dreamed metaphors for MPD such as "There was another spirit living in my body" or "I dreamed I was twins." Many met their alters first as dream characters. In the case study *Sybil,* the patient dreams of being introduced to fifteen children who turn out to be her alters. Multiples in my study had dreams in which several alters met and interacted, each remembering signal events from the perspective of a different dream character. Some alters orchestrate dreams for the host to influence her, such as causing nightmares about a friend with whom the alter had decided the host should not get too intimate. Hosts also sometimes remembered something as a dream that turned out to have been an alter's real experience. One patient in the study, who had recurring "nightmares" of catching evil cats by the throat and stuffing them in garbage cans, awoke from one of these dreams to find the velour jogging suit in which she slept covered in very real feline hair. She did not own a cat.

The following week, Terese reported that the tape and the Muses helped her to sleep even better than the pills. Her nightmares had stopped. "I did have one dream that was about the stuff with my father, but it wasn't the same literal flashback. I had some control. It was actually a good dream in a weird way. Do you want to hear it?" she asked.

"Yes, as long as there's nothing more urgent. We can talk about the dream and even do some interpretation of it with hypnosis if you'd like."

"Yes, it's the most interesting thing I can think of. Everything else is okay. My brother paid to get the piano tuned after the move, so I got to start practicing this week. Day treatment is fine—maybe a little boring, but they're already talking about letting me cut back my hours there. And like I said, I'm sleeping fine."

"Okay then, why don't you tell me the dream?"

"Well, in the dream there was a corporation that my father ran that sold meat at some kind of carnival, like an amusement park with rides. He sold these big slabs of meat." Terese grimaced. "They were gross and bloody, and he was trying to fry them up and give them to people to eat. I'm a vegetarian anyway, but I discovered that it was human meat and I had to stop him. There was a big knife that he used for cutting up the meat. I took it and stabbed him, and he fell down dead.

"Then, in the dream, I knew that I had to kill myself," she continued more calmly. "The scene changed and I walked out of a building with my brother leading the way. I was a martyr dressed in a long black robe. We walked through a beautiful garden and down to a river. There were little boats about six feet long and my brother indicated I should get into one. I lay down in it and folded my hands over my heart and began to float downstream. This was death, this was how it was done."

I recognized elements of Patti and Joan in Terese's scenario. Terese's perspective shifted from one to the other. This was a good sign that they were no longer totally dissociated from her. It is also encouraging when trauma survivors move from dreaming a simple reenactment of the event (in this case, Terese's memory of her father cooking "human" meat) to a different outcome involving a sense of mastery. This is true even when the outcome is an undesirable outcome for waking life, such as the stabbing. Dreams are, after all, metaphoric. Dreaming of death can also be a metaphor for an outmoded part of the self dying off. However, given that Joan was often suicidal, it seemed likely that the romanticized depiction was of literal death.

"You seem close to both Patti and Joan in this dream," I observed.

"Yes, it was like I *was* Patti, seeing her usual perception. Then, when I killed my dad, I was still Patti, but also myself. We were one. Then I was Joan, she's always dressed like I was in the dream, in a black robe."

"Would you like to go back into the dream using hypnosis to explore it?" I asked her.

"Yes, that sounds interesting."

I did a brief induction and started to make suggestions about the dream. "You can begin to picture yourself there. You are at a carnival, like an amusement park with rides."

"Oui. C'est un corporation," she responded. *"Il vende la viande. C'est humaine."* Her eyes popped open, and she stared in terror at the corner of my office, as if seeing someone there. *"Il est ici!"*

"Can you speak English so I can follow you?"

"Aide moi! Aide moi!"

"Oui, Patti," I managed. I searched for other words, remembering *la bouteille* was "bottle." I hoped that was close enough to flask. *"Ton Papa en bouteille. Ferme les yeux, s'il tu plait."* Terese obligingly squeezed her lids shut and grimaced as if concentrating on the imagery. *"Maintenant, ferme la bouteille."* I figured "close the bottle" was pretty close to what a five-year-old would say for 'cork the flask' anyway. She relaxed.

"Now, Terese, if you hear me, see whether you can be here without Patti leaving. Just come and be one with her like in your dream. Then think about what you'd like to do about your father."

"Yes, we're both here. I'm her—or she's me. I don't need to do anything else about my dad. He's in the bottle that's floated way out to sea. That means it's in the past. I know the meat was a long time ago even though I remember it myself."

"Can Patti understand me? Do I need to speak French, too?"

"No, we really are one person. I can speak French now. *Français ou anglais*—either one!"

"Let's move to the part of the dream where you're Joan. See yourself as a martyr dressed in black heading through the garden for the boat. Why are you thinking about dying?"

"I'm guilty," she said somberly, adopting some of Joan's persona but continuing to speak in English. "I wanted to kill my father. That's a mortal sin, and I must die as punishment."

"But now all you've done is lock your father away in the past. Don't you think it might be okay to live, even to be happy?"

"I need to die for what I did to my brother, too."

"You mentioned that once before. What exactly do you mean?"

"When we lived in Paris, my father was doing sexual things to me." Her voice retained the calm sadness of Joan. "I would take my brother down to the basement of that house and make him do the same things."

"You mean you would do what your father did, or your brother would act out your father's role?"

"Both. Sometimes I'd stick something in him. Usually I'd make him pretend to be Papa and stick things in me. He wouldn't want to. He knew it was wrong and that it hurt me. I knew he hated it but I'd make him. I was **three** years older and he'd do anything I said. I was abusing him."

"Are you sure that's a real memory?"

"Yes," she said solemnly. "I'm sure."

"Have you ever talked about it with him?"

"Yes, I tried to apologize. Either he didn't remember it or he wouldn't acknowledge it. He said whatever I might have done, that he forgave me. He knows my childhood was even worse than his. My father and uncle are the ones he blames for everything that went on when we were children."

It is common for children to act out with dolls what has been done to them. Normal children may be overheard identifying with a powerful adult in "cute" conversations scolding their dolls. They tell them they were bad dolls and must stay after school or can't go outside to play. Traumatized children can be observed acting out their horrifying versions of this. They may tell a baby doll that because she was bad, a male doll is going to put his "thing" between her legs or that someone will burn her with a cigarette.

This was not the first time I'd heard of such trauma enactment extending to a younger sibling. Obviously, it was a tragedy, but I wanted to reinforce her brother's generous advice. "That sounds reasonable. No one would expect a child of what—seven? eight?—to figure out what's right or wrong when an adult is doing that to her. Your brother forgives you, and the church teaches that God forgives, why don't you forgive yourself?"

"I'll think about it," she pronounced tentatively. This seemed like the best we were going to do right now.

"Okay. Why don't you begin to leave the dream and the thoughts that go with it far behind as you start to wake up?" With many multiples, trance is not a distinctly different state from normal consciousness. I wasn't sure it was necessary, but I counted Terese awake.

"How do you feel?" I asked.

"I think I'm integrated with Patti; I'm not sure if it's for good, but we seem to be the same person. I remember what it was like to have the flashbacks about my father and the meat. I know French all of a sudden. A year ago, I integrated an alter. I used to have a tough-guy one who had come into existence when my uncle tried to strangle us. That alter would be around only if someone was threatened. Last year, I worked on that memory, and he became me. Then I could physically defend myself and didn't need to 'switch.' It feels like maybe that happened with Patti."

There are many ways alters can be integrated. Psychiatrist Richard Kluft has devised poetic hypnotic rituals to help people with MPD say good-bye to their individual alters and have them merge—after the foundation has been laid by exploration of the original cause of the split. Christine Costner Sizemore, the multiple personality described in *The Three Faces of Eve,* reports that—contrary to the book—she integrated years later in a dream of a temple ceremony to bid her alters farewell. Most of the integrations I've facilitated have arisen spontaneously while pursuing broader therapeutic goals. I'd been trying to get Terese in touch with Patti's perspective but hadn't expected this exercise would be her final appearance.

It did seem over the following sessions that Patti was fully integrated into Terese. Joan remained separate, enjoying the fact that Terese now conversed with her in French. A few weeks later, Terese brought me two parcels wrapped in black felt. They turned out to be small stained-glass windows that Joan had just made. One depicted a man's disembodied face and phallus menacing a small girl, whose expression was reminiscent of the one in Edvard Munch's *Scream*. The other depicted girl's and boy's horrified faces, separated by a phallic object.

Despite the unsettling theme, the windows were cut from deep tones of red and purple glass and authentically leaded for an eerie resemblance to cathedral biblical scenes.

"Joan has decided that penance might suffice for her sins without having to die," Terese told me. I wanted to get her away from the guilt eventually, but her current attitude seemed a large improvement. She had been able to work with the large shards of glass without incident, whereas in the past this had precipitated a suicide attempt and hospitalization.

In the following weeks, I interacted with various of Terese's alters. Kenny provoked a series of crises with one of his long-standing habits. He felt cramped in many settings—the day treatment center, the new apartment. His reaction was to run out, climb the tallest tree he could find, and hide there. When he eventually wanted to get down, he would "switch" and let Terese deal with navigating them out of their precarious position. In hypnosis, I managed to persuade him to restrict this maneuver to their imaginary clearing.

Veronica, the shy adolescent who dealt with nonviolent sexual situations, and Joseph, who had little language, never emerged to talk to me. However, we modified the relaxation tapes to accommodate them. I continued to hear news of Carli and Herman, her pig, who was healthy and happy with his mistress mostly to himself. Terese drifted back to spending the majority of her time with her musician friends. Day treatment cut her down to twice a week so that she could practice the piano more seriously. Three months after her hospitalization, Terese was invited to go on a concert tour. After that, she was thinking of settling at a music conservatory in the Southwest. "They're offering me a fellowship, and I can earn money tutoring their undergraduates. I should get a master's degree for the best teaching jobs. I can't count on earning a decent living from performing. Only a few pianists in the world do. I don't want to keep letting my brother subsidize me." We made a tape rehearsing being calm during her performances to be on the safe side. However, the stage, so often an enormous stressor for other musicians, had always been a positive refuge for Terese.

In our final session, Joan came out to tell me that the clearing she visualized to calm herself now sported an angel statue that looked like me. Kenny said that he would think of me in his treetop. Veronica and Joseph just passed along "good-bye" messages. Terese herself was cheerful about her upcoming tour. I gave her a referral to someone in Santa Fe and wished her the best.

Two weeks later, I saw an announcement in *The New York Times* for one of her performances. After some months, there was a smaller one for a concert at the conservatory.

The ideal outcome for multiple personality disorder is to integrate. That leaves the person less vulnerable to disturbing symptoms in the future. However, some multiples stabilize well simply by gaining conscious control over switching and by learning effective communication among parts of the self.

When I do hypnosis for a simple phobia, weight loss, or insomnia, I am usually the first and last therapist the patient will see. However, people suffering from MPD and other complex disorders typically do not begin and complete treatment with the same therapist—although I often see them longer than Terese. During my training, it was I who was regularly departing for somewhere else; now it is the patients. Managed care also contributes by switching the group of providers whose treatment is covered. Some patients benefit from exposure to several therapists with different approaches. However, most of the time they are helped despite, not because of, these shifts.

On the few occasions when I've been the first to diagnose multiple personality, with the exception of Dolores, I've carried out the tasks of helping patients understand their blackouts or voices and establishing some cooperation between alters. More often, as a hypnotherapist, I see patients who are referred after the diagnosis and treatment has begun—as I've said, hypnosis is especially effective with these trancelike disorders. I've followed some of these latter-stage multiples through to their final integration. They typically relinquish the intense extremes of some alters—adorable child, drama queen, unflappable stoic—but one sees bits of all these in the more complete person, just as we all show more than one face to the world. I hope someday Terese will have all her remarkable creativity within one identity.

7
The Writer Who Couldn't Read

The alien abduction craze was just beginning at the time I first heard from Joseph Gold's parents. One of my colleagues at Harvard Medical School, John Mack, had written a popular book on the topic and given a hospital colloquium positing abductions as an unrecognized cause of much psychopathology. Harvard deans and department chairs grumbled about whether this was a legitimate exercise of academic freedom—after much debate, they grudgingly allowed it. Down the street, MIT hosted the first international conference on alien abductions and was soon scrambling to explain to skeptical journalists that they granted space to any meeting a faculty member chaired.

Every licensed psychologist and psychiatrist in Massachusetts received a free book detailing a Roper poll funded anonymously. The scion of a major philanthropic family was quickly identified as the source. The book deemed sleep paralysis, amnesiac spells, and seeing balls of light as signs suggestive of alien abduction. Twenty-one percent of the population reported at least one of these signs and 2 percent reported four or more—the book's criteria for probably having been abducted. Abduction enthusiasts used hypnotic questioning in an extremely leading manner. ("Do you see a spaceship? Is there any kind of being there?") The favorite joke around the medical school ended with a punch line suggesting the False Memory Syndrome Foundation had funded the research. FMSF couldn't have bought better publicity to disparage the concept of repression of traumatic memories.

One spring afternoon, my answering machine showed four messages. The first was from Dr. Ernest Hartmann, the leading sleep disorder specialist in Boston. "I've referred you a very interesting patient. His name is Joseph Gold. I saw him last year for nightmares and some kind of seizures. Now he's in the hospital and can't talk, read, or write. The doctors there think it's psychosomatic. His parents want me to see him. I thought you might try hypnosis at the same time. I gave them your number."

The second was a female voice. "This is Mrs. Gold. We were referred to you for hypnosis with our son. He's in the hospital following a seizure or stroke or pseudoseizure—his doctors can't decide. He can't read or write and he's supposed to take his finals and graduate from Harvard in a few weeks. Please call me back as soon as possible." She left the number of a posh Boston hotel.

The third message was also Mrs. Gold. "I'm calling about my son. Ernest Hartmann gave us your name. Our son Joseph has had some kind of seizure or something and can't read or write. Please call me." The machine recorded a third, nearly identical message from her half an hour later. I wondered if Mrs. Gold intentionally repeated the basics assuming her message wasn't getting through. There was no hint of impatience in her pleasant voice, although the frequency of her calls suggested otherwise.

I dialed Dr. Hartmann, hoping to get more information on the referral. His answering machine picked up, so I left a message. I called the Golds' hotel. Mrs. Gold was effusively pleased to hear from me. After repeating once more the information she'd left in the phone messages, she went on to describe the episode in which her son had lost the ability to speak, read, or write. The doctors had originally thought that Joseph had suffered a stroke, but after three days of neurological workups, they'd decided that it must be psychological. As a parent, Mrs. Gold worried that they might be missing something and encouraged them to do more tests. However, she also acknowledged that they should pursue psychological possibilities. She was calling me to make the appointment because Joseph's speech was still limited, although improving, after two weeks of speech therapy. He was eager to see me and to do anything Dr. Hartmann recommended. Hartmann had spoken highly of me. Mrs. Gold was charming and flattering without overdoing it. She showed a commendable awareness of the issues in arranging treatment for an adult son. We made the appointment for three days hence. Although Joseph had absolutely no ability to read or write even individual letters, she said his speech was progressing rapidly. He would be able to talk to me adequately by then.

Late afternoon, Ernest Hartmann called back. "I saw Joseph last year for three months," he told me. "He was having terrible nightmares and had read my book on the topic. The description of nightmare sufferers as sensitive and creative resonated for him, although his dreams were very unusual—all about what he called the 'White People.' Not just as in Caucasian. His 'White People' are bald, naked, and snowy white. He'd go to sleep and they'd appear standing in front of a movie screen. Dreadful images were on the screen. We had him sleep in the lab and found these weren't your usual REM nightmares." I knew from research by Hartmann and others that nightmares usually occur in Rapid Eye Movement (REM) sleep—the stage for most dreams. REM generally doesn't begin until ninety minutes into sleep.

"Joseph's episodes began at sleep onset, just a minute or two into Stage I non-REM. He had daytime hallucinations that might have been seizures. During these he'd see the White People just standing or walking around wherever he was. I wondered if what he described as nightmares could also be seizures that occurred during sleep. There wasn't any abnormality in his EEG, but as we know, temporal lobe problems can be very hard to detect." Temporal lobe seizures often result in strange sensory perceptions rather than the motor spasms or unconsciousness we more typically think of as epilepsy.

"I prescribed Tegretol just to see if it would help," Dr. Hartmann continued, referring to the most common temporal lobe seizure medication. "I thought it made the nightmares less frequent, although Joseph didn't seem to think it helped. He stopped seeing me and must have run out of medication pretty soon. Now he's had what looked like a grand mal seizure, but they can't find a physical cause. I still think it might be an atypical seizure, and I'm wondering about Tegretol again. The other possibility is that it's a conversion reaction. Would hypnosis be able to tell much about that?"

Conversion reactions, as I explained in relation to Nancy's light switch hallucinations, are perceptual or motor symptoms that are psychologically caused. I told him it was likely to illuminate this quickly. Most people with dissociation and conversion disorders—such as pseudo-seizures—are highly hypnotizable. We compared notes and found that Dr. Hartmann's appointment with Joseph was earlier on the same day as mine. The Golds were bringing medical records and some of Joseph's writing from before the seizure. Dr. Hartmann would send these materials along to me after perusing them himself.

Three days later, Joseph arrived with his father, who was pleasant although less outgoing than his wife. Joseph was a handsome young man with black hair and expressive hazel eyes. His voice, in contrast, was bland and flat during our opening small talk—the aftermath of his medical crisis—but he spoke well enough that I could understand him and get answers to my questions. First we needed privacy. I offered Joseph's father the choice of a small TV room, which I use as the waiting area in my home office, or directions to Harvard Square. I'm five minutes from the prime tourist area—bookstores, historic sites, street performers. Mr. Gold knew the square from other visits to Joseph and set off for his favorite stores.

"I talked to your mother and Dr. Hartmann," I told Joseph once we were settled in my office. "But I'd still like to hear the whole story from you."

"It started with this seizure . . . or they say now maybe it wasn't a seizure," Joseph replied in his expressionless monotone. "There was only a week of classes remaining. What they ironically call "reading days" is most of what I've missed. I had already turned in two term papers and the poems for my directed study in creative writing. Dr. Hartmann has a copy of the poems. I said he could pass them along to you with all the CAT scans and EEG's. That week I'd gotten notification that I won a fellowship to a writers' retreat out west. It will pay me to write a novel next year, which is what I really want to do. I also got a letter from my girlfriend—odd since she lives just across the 'quad.' She said she wanted to break up." There was still no hint of emotion in his voice. "I didn't want to, but it had gotten to be a pretty stormy relationship. Maybe it's for the best."

Joseph continued with a narrative of the actual incident. He'd sat down at his computer to write. There his memory went blank. His suite mate heard a loud crash and ran into the room. He'd found Joseph on the floor in front of the desk, unconscious but twitching spasmodically. By the time the other young man had called an ambulance, Joseph was regaining consciousness. When confronted with a barrage of "What happened? Are you all right?" Joseph was unable to find any words to answer. Finally, he was able to whisper "Henry"—the name of a character in a movie they had recently seen who was trapped incommunicado in a body with his mind still intact. His roommate was reassured by the allusion and hastened to explain it to the paramedics upon their arrival.

The ambulance rushed him to the emergency room where Joseph was given a CAT scan to determine whether his brain showed the bleeding of a stroke—it did not. His EEG had no sign of an ongoing seizure either. He was admitted to a neurology unit to begin the slower procedures of blood profiles, reflex testing, and EEG "evoke potentials" to tell if he might be in a postseizure state. In the first twenty-four hours, Joseph managed a few labored yes and no responses to questions. The first time the speech therapist visited him, she was able to teach him to produce other sounds, and his vocabulary started to return. However, from the moment he had regained consciousness in his room, Joseph could not read or write. Meaningless symbols labeled everything around him and he could not begin to fathom how to move the pencils that were repeatedly thrust into his hand.

"English looks like hieroglyphics," he told me. "You can see that there is a pattern or intent to it that is different from random scratches. I can recognize the unit of a word by the larger spaces between marks, but it might as well be a code into which I have not been initiated. At least my voice is coming back fast. Even three days ago, I spoke like some bad computer synthesizer with absolutely no accent on syllables. My friends still tell me I don't sound like myself, but strangers don't stare like there's anything wrong anymore."

I took notes. Each time I looked down at my paper, and attended only to his voice, Joseph sounded as if he had no feelings about any of this. When I looked up, all manner of subtle signals of anxiety, sadness, warmth, and humor danced across his face.

I wanted to hear his version of the earlier problems. "Dr. Hartmann told me about the White People dreams and visions," I said, striving for a polite term. "Can you describe the White People to me?"

"They're white as if paint had been poured on them—in terms of their color and also their skin is smooth with no pores, almost plastic. They're completely nude and bald." He continued in his precise, expressionless way. "There are men and women—probably about equal numbers over time. They're all young adults; there are no children or old people. They look humanoid, but not quite human. They're solemn most of the time."

"And in the dreams, there are movie screens?"

"Yes, that's what's scary—what's on the screen, not the White People. The White People just gesture at the screen like Vanna White." His face signaled the irony that his voice lacked.

"What's on the screens that's so awful?"

"It's always something violent. Usually I'm in the scene doing the violence. Once in a while, there's just some atrocity without me there."

"Can you give me examples?"

"Well, the violence is always toward babies or young women. I might be a doctor who's just delivered an infant. When they hand me the scalpel to cut the umbilical cord, I slice open the baby instead. Or there's one where a young woman's arm has been cut lengthways all the way down to the bone. I've told her that I called help. She's expecting an ambulance to be there soon, but I haven't made any call. I'm just watching her bleed to death." He winced as his voice continued expressionlessly. "In some dreams, I rape a woman before killing her."

The degree of violence Joseph described led me to ask, "Have you ever had any traumas in waking life?"

"No."

"Do you have any brothers or sisters?"

"Yes, I have a sister, Penny. She's a year and half younger than me, and we're very good friends." I'd been wondering about siblings who died in infancy, but apparently not.

"Has anything happened in waking life that reminds you of your dreams?"

"Thankfully not."

"Do you have other sleep problems?"

"I have insomnia in the sense that it's hard to go to sleep when I'm having the nightmares a lot."

"Anything else? Do you ever walk or talk in your sleep?"

"I've been told I talk in my sleep." Joseph paused, sounding reluctant for the first time. "During these dreams mostly."

"What do you say?"

"I, uh, really don't know. You'd have to ask my old girlfriend, Erica. She's said she'd be happy to talk to doctors. I don't think anyone has called." He recited the number from memory, and I wrote it next to the phrase "talks in sleep."

"Dr. Hartmann said that when he put you on Tegretol, he thought the nightmares got better. But you didn't agree?"

"The nightmares were less frequent then, but I didn't believe it had anything to do with Tegretol. After I stopped taking it, they continued getting better."

"Do you have another idea about why they decreased?"

He hesitated a moment. "Well, I came to believe there might be some veridical reality to the White People. I began to talk to them. I'd tell them I didn't like the nightmares, ask them why they were visiting me."

"Did they answer?" I asked as neutrally as possible.

"Not directly. I wasn't hearing voices, if that's what you mean. But I believed they might be understanding and trying to modulate their appearances to me. The nightmares did get a lot better."

"If the White People have some 'veridical reality,'" I asked, adopting Joseph's terminology, "what might they be?"

"I guess a kind of entity on another plane of existence. I know that probably sounds silly to you, but it seemed like at least a possibility I should consider."

"And what do you believe about them now?"

"I don't know. They might be the product of some seizure-like activity, as Dr. Hartmann suggested. They could be psychological—a part of me—I gather that's what the hypnosis referral is supposed to tell. . . . . Or they might be real. I'm keeping an open mind these days."

"What do you think caused you to lose your reading and writing?"

"I'm keeping an open mind on that one too. Stroke, seizure, psychological . . . or something else."

"Have you wondered if the White People may have

. . . er . . . taken your language?" I asked. This seemed a logical corollary if one believed they were real.

"That thought has crossed my mind," he said guardedly, seeming to watch my response.

"Any idea why they'd do that?"

"They might be using it for some purpose of their own—studying it or learning to write." He smiled a bit—but only a bit—sheepishly. Joseph was obviously not one to defer to authority, especially when the authorities didn't even agree with each other. Despite his stated agnosticism, I sensed he favored the White People's existence.

Before we had time to explore any of the numerous other intriguing lines of questioning, the hour was up and Joseph's father was returning to collect him. In his hand was the remains of an exotic Caribbean cigar. He joked good-naturedly with Joseph about evading Mrs. Gold's prohibitions against smoking. They told me that Joseph would be coming to future appointments on his own. His dorm was an easy walk from my office. His parents planned to return to their home in coastal Maine later that week. Joseph and I made an appointment for the following Thursday.

On Monday, a thick envelope arrived from Dr. Hartmann. One metal clip bound photocopies of the hospital's records. Another held pages of poetry. I leafed through the hospital emergency room notes. The admitting exam said the symptoms suggested a postseizure syndrome. There were elaborate charts and images documenting brain scans and EEG's. These were eventually judged not consistent with "alexia" and "agraphia"—the medical terms for losing your spoken and written language respectively. Later diagnostic impressions referred first to "atypical postseizure symptoms" and later to "pseudoseizures."

Then Joseph's history of hallucinations was emphasized and the word *psychotic* appeared in the records. It was hard to tell the full import of this—some neurologists misuse this term to mean "psychological." However, the last entries did seem to employ it to suggest that Joseph was out of touch with reality. The psychologists who had tested him called him "narcissistic," which could have been a genuine psychiatric observation or an informal comment that they found him condescending and arrogant, since he'd indicated that he planned to leave the hospital before they recommended. I was discouraged to see this familiar equation of hallucination with psychosis. As I've mentioned in other chapters, hallucinations are common in both dissociation and other milder disorders as well as in imaginative and highly hypnotizable people with no disorder. Joseph certainly had none of the disorganization of thinking or incomprehension of social norms that accompany psychosis.

The second stack of papers made for better reading. Joseph's poetry had a sinister tone, although much of it was dark humor. The longest poem was titled "The Company." It described a business where mundane events happen. Every action was ingeniously made to sound ominous by its overly studied normality. Suspense built and built without resolution—as is allowed only in poetry. One could see Joseph had talent but it was hard to tell what else to make of his poetry.

Erica, Joseph's ex-girlfriend, answered on the second ring when I phoned her. "Hi, I'm Deirdre Barrett, a psychologist," I said. "Joseph Gold suggested you might be able to give me some information about him."

"I was wondering when someone was going to call."

"He's told me about the White People he saw in his dreams and sometimes awake. The thing he told me you might know more about was whether he talks in his sleep—does he?"

"Well, it's not exactly Joseph that talks."

"What?"

"Someone else—or something else—talks when he's asleep."

"What does he . . . it say?"

"The most common thing is he'd breath in gasps, like he was having a bad dream, and I'd call his name. He'd say, 'He's not here!' in this awful voice, like something demonic or maybe more like a machine. It didn't sound human. 'He's not here,'" she hissed in a spine-chilling imitation, much like Linda Blair in *The Exorcist*. "That's not very close. It's so weird I can't imitate them." I noticed the change in pronoun but let it pass for a moment. "They'd say, 'Don't worry,' or 'He's safe' and 'He'll be coming back.' Then if I'd ask them questions, they would answer, but always as if struggling to find each word, like they didn't speak English naturally and had to translate. They'd use odd grammatical constructions too."

"You say 'they.' Who do you mean?"

"Well, the White People."

"From his dreams?"

"Yes. They were supposed to be not quite human and very detached. That's how the voice sounded. They weren't just in the dreams. He'd see them sometimes awake. He'd look at some point in the room, really focusing on it. I'd feel like there was actually something there."

"What would you ask these White People?"

"Philosophical questions—what they were there for. And I know it sounds crazy, but I'd ask them if they would appear to me. When I was with Joseph, I came to believe that they existed. It was very compelling, the way he described them and that voice. I felt something special was happening to him and I didn't want to be left out. That sounds silly to me now." I was getting very practiced at taking a belief in these "White People" in stride.

"What did they say about your wanting to see them?"

"They told me it wasn't allowed—that their purpose was with Joseph. I had thought maybe I was involved because sometimes I was in the dreams."

"What was your role in the dreams?"

"In some of them, he was raping or killing me." Joseph hadn't mentioned this detail.

"Did he ever walk in his sleep, or move in any way during all this?"

"No, he was always still on his back, except for the awful breathing. He looked sound asleep even when he spoke. It was like they were just using his vocal cords."

"Is there anything else you think I should know?"

"No, I just hope he gets better. He's a wonderful person." It seemed intrusive to ask why she had broken up with this "wonderful person." Some young women would have been frightened away by the dreams, but she had sounded unthreatened, even intrigued by them.

"Erica says when you talk in your sleep it's like the White People, that you say things like 'He's not here.' " I told Joseph in our next session.

"Yeah, I think maybe she told me something like that," he replied briskly.

"You sound like you don't want to talk about it."

"It seems kind of creepy." I could hear mild apprehension in his voice; his speech had clearly progressed.

"Erica said some of the dreams were about you hurting her."

"Yes. It seems a little scary now that I was sleeping next to her while having those violent dreams. But she wasn't concerned about it."

I dropped the topic of the conversation with Erica and questioned him about his reading and writing. Although it might be as disturbing a symptom to someone else as the sleep-talking, he didn't seem to have the same "creepy" associations about not being able to recognize even a letter of the alphabet.

"Today I'd like to do some hypnosis with you. It may help us to figure out if all of this is psychological."

Joseph was agreeable and I did an induction. He relaxed quickly and appeared to be in trance. "I want you to begin to let yourself move back in time. You can imagine that you are looking at the hands of a clock face. They slowly start to rotate backward. Watch them turning faster now, so that they're just a blur. You can feel yourself pulled back in time until you stop at some pleasant point just before your 'seizure.' Just feel yourself stopping at this point before the seizure, and then you can look around in your mind's eye to survey the scene. You are going to be able to tell me where you are and what you are doing while remaining deeply asleep."

"I'm sitting outside on the steps of Widener Library. I'm reading through my poem, trying to decide what should go in the third stanza. 'The Company . . .' " He began to recite the piece I'd read as a finished work.

"Can you see the words in front of you?"

"Yes, I've written in blue pen on unlined paper."

"Good. In a minute, I am going to ask you to copy a few lines of that poem. I'll hand you a pen and paper. You can keep your eyes closed or open them, as you wish. You will write on the paper while remaining in a deep sleeplike state." I handed him a pen and legal pad. "Okay, now write the first stanza of the poem."

Joseph's eyes opened just a crack. They were directed at the notepad, but they did not appear to be clearly focused on it. He began to write. His handwriting was messy because he was holding the pen loosely, but the words were legible. His movements were so sluggish that it took him a couple of minutes to write the four short lines.

"Okay, you can close your eyes now and continue to sleep deeply. When you awaken, you will remember as much as you want to of what we have done clearly and in detail. If you are ready to, you may even choose to bring your ability to read and write back with you," I suggested tentatively. "But for now, let the scene of working on your poem fade from your mind's eye as you come back to the present time. I am going to count backwards

from ten. By the count of one you will be wide awake."
As I said the numbers slowly, Joseph visibly regained muscle tone. At "one," he started awake.

"What do you remember?" I asked.

"Something really vague about sitting outside the library."

"Can you read this?" I held up the pad in front of him.

"No."

"Any idea what it is?"

"Did I write that?"

"Yes, do you remember?"

"No. It just makes sense that's the only reason you'd
be showing it to me now."

"Being able to write in trance does suggest that the
cause is psychological."

Joseph responded only with a noncommittal "Hmmm"—
more commonly stereotyped as the therapist's side of a conversation.

"I know people don't like to be told it's psychological," I continued. "But it's actually good news. You *really*
don't want to have something physically wrong with your
brain. That's much less easily fixable. Writing in trance is
a strong sign that you will get it back completely."

"Couldn't hypnosis affect a symptom even if it's physical?"

"It's very unlikely. The only neurological problems
that hypnosis affects are ones that anxiety aggravates—
and hypnosis improves the anxious part only. For example, stutterers with both speech phobia and organic
damage may not stutter in trance anything like they do
when awake and nervous. However, your writing isn't that
sort of subtle difference. It's pretty all-or-nothing." I won-

dered what he might be thinking about how hypnosis would interact with the White-People-stole-my-writing hypothesis. Could trance induce them to loan it back temporarily?

"So what's next?" Joseph asked.

I told him I wanted to use the following several hypnotic sessions to explore why he had developed the symptom. I also said I'd make more suggestions that might begin to help Joseph carry over his writing into the waking state.

Later that afternoon, I told Ernest Hartmann that Joseph had written in trance. He asked almost the same question as Joseph had about whether this could be possible with an organic symptom. I described in even more detail why I thought not in this case. "Also, he had amnesia for hypnosis without my suggesting it," I added. "He says he doesn't have a trauma history, but the amnesia, the conversion disorder, and the dream content all sound like he might."

"I can't imagine that," Dr. Hartmann replied. "His parents seem so nice." This was my impression of them also, but I've become very cynical after years of seeing patients like Nancy and Marie. "Even if it's a conversion reaction, I'd wonder whether that and the dream content might be about sibling rivalry. It's always young women and babies he hurts. He's got a younger sister. He says he's very close to her, but she displaced his only child status, so there could be some issues." His sister sounded to me like the only person he'd mentioned in an unambivalently positive light. I do think conversion reactions and dissociative disorders are linked to childhood trauma. However, there is a body of literature on "vulnerability" to trauma suggesting that some people are susceptible to lesser stresses than others. Symptoms are not always proportional to the objective severity of the event. There is also much research on the broad array of hallucinations and odd personality symptoms that can accompany temporal lobe seizures. People can see visions, smell strange odors or develop very odd religious beliefs when they have repeated bursts of abnormal electrical activity in this area. Dr. Hartmann told me he was suggesting that Joseph consider taking Tegretol again. Since no one was sure what was going on, I supposed it wouldn't hurt to pursue all avenues.

In my next session with Joseph, I did hypnosis again. "Focus on your inability to read and write," I suggested once he was in a trance. "Think about how incomprehensible words look. Let that form a bridge to some other place and time that might tell you something about why this is. Just feel yourself moving to that other scene that has something to do with losing your language."

"Green," Joseph moaned in a soft, childlike voice.

"Green?" I asked. "What else do you see?"

"Just green. . . . My head hurts," he continued in the same plaintive voice. "It hurts bad."

"Where does it hurt?"

"In back. . . . Hurts."

"Where are you?"

"Green. . . . My head!"

Joseph made several low moans. He seemed increasingly distressed and less responsive to my inquiries. I decided this was all that could be learned of the scene for now, even though I did not understand its connection to his symptoms. I suggested he leave it behind and moved him to the memory on the library steps. I had him practice writing in trance again before I awakened him.

"Do you remember what we just did?"

"Maybe something about the library again?"

"Anything else?"

"No."

"You said something about 'green' and your 'head hurt.' Does that mean anything to you?"

"No," he said with little emotion. He had no waking memory of what he had been picturing in trance. Even when I talked more about it, he couldn't connect it with his language problems. I asked him if there were any incidents in childhood that did remind him of his present difficulties.

"There was one thing that I keep feeling like has something to do with the White People—although it didn't actually involve them. When I was little, we used to drive to this beach. I remember one time we went there; on the way there was a big black bird that flew low toward the car. I don't know how to describe this, but it's like my memory splits into two realities. In one, the bird narrowly missed the car and we kept driving. In the other, the bird hit and splattered all over the windshield. My father got out of the car and opened the trunk. He took my beach towel and used it to wipe the blood and feathers off the windshield. I was upset about the bird but I was also upset about my towel. I have both these memories—of the bird hitting and the bird missing the car—as if they both happened in two parallel universes."

It seemed to me likelier that a dissociative child would imagine the benign scenario to mask the upsetting one, but either was possible. I really didn't know what to make of the strange memory, so I explored Joseph's understanding of it. "You said you felt like that might be related to the White People—in what way?"

"It just had the same feeling that seeing them many years later did. It was as if a tear in the fabric of the universe opened that they were later able to come through."

We ended the session on that puzzling note.

Friday I had a message from Mrs. Gold asking me to call her. "I wanted to know how Joseph is doing," she began warmly when we connected by phone.

"Pretty good. He's not writing yet, but it looks like there's nothing wrong neurologically. I'm optimistic about the symptoms going away." In as pleasant a tone as possible, I added, "I really can't tell you much else without formal permission from Joseph. We haven't talked about what he wants shared. Everything is automatically confidential unless he says otherwise. If you have anything you want to tell me, I'm happy to listen though."

"Oh, I understand completely," she said. "I wouldn't want to intrude. After all, he's a grown-up young man. We sort of *had* to talk to his doctors when he couldn't read, write, *or* speak. But now that he's improved, I'm sure it's better for him to handle it on his own without his parents looking over his shoulder. I guess the habits of motherhood just die hard. He has been filling me in; he told me that he'd written something during hypnosis. That's really good, isn't it?"

"Yes," I said guardedly, not wanting to encourage more questions.

"I called mostly to say how grateful we are that you're helping. Nothing else was the least bit effective so far, and it sounds like you're doing such a great job! And Dr. Hartmann's wonderful, too, of course. I'm not sure anyone at the hospital knew what they were doing. I'm so glad he's in good hands now."

"Well, thank you," I said, feeling flattered but vaguely uneasy. Logically her you're-number-one-and-your-friend-is-a-close-second, no-one-else-is-in-the-ballpark message was a bit heavy-handed. However, her tone was so warm and sincere that it was tempting to take it at face value.

"Joseph asked me to tell you what I knew about that story about the bird. But it didn't happen."

"Do you remember the incident?" I asked her.

"No, but I would know if a bird ever hit our windshield." She explained with concern, "In a car with two small children, something like that certainly would have stuck with me."

She continued without prompting. "I've wracked my brain for anything that might have been traumatic—either psychological or physical. The neurology people kept asking about blows to the head. There were only two that I know of—neither one too bad. One happened at camp when he was six or seven. They called me to come get him. He'd fallen out of a tree, and they thought he'd been unconscious for a minute. He was complaining of a headache." I thought of his trance comments. Green grass? Green leaves? "I took him straight to the doctor's. They said he had a mild concussion and to keep him in bed for a few days.

"The other time was even more minor. He fell off a swing set in the neighbors' yard. He hit his head on the ground and bruised it but didn't lose consciousness. The doctor said it was nothing; he didn't even have to stay in bed. I just don't know of anything bad enough to cause seizures."

"Well, thank you for calling." I began to conclude our conversation. "This has been helpful."

"Ummm . . ." This was often the moment callers got to their point. "I wanted to ask you one more thing. I don't know if you can tell me or not, but it's been bothering me."

"I'm not able to talk about the content of the sessions without consulting with Joseph first." I ended the statement on a questioning intonation, inviting her to specify what I was declining to answer. I was indeed curious what was "bothering" her.

"Has Joseph said anything about being abused as a child?" she asked. This was even more intriguing than I'd expected.

"Why do you ask?" I parlayed, with the classic analyst's response to questions. I couldn't imagine what she would say to this given her denial of any other traumas minutes earlier.

"When the family therapist at the hospital asked him if he was ever abused as a child he said yes. They didn't ask him anything more, at least not in that session. I didn't feel like I could ask. I just wondered if he'd told you about that."

"No, he didn't mention the family session," I said, purposely obtuse—I knew that was not the main point she was asking. "What did you think he was referring to?"

"I have no idea. I was just amazed. I've been trying to figure it out ever since."

"Like I said, I'd need to get his permission to talk with

you in detail even if I do ask him about that." I wasn't sure what information I was protecting. Had he told me about abuse? "Green . . . head hurts"—not clearly at least.

"No, please don't even mention I asked. Just forget about it. I'm sure it was nothing."

I thanked her again for calling. She repeated her praise briefly and seemed eager to end the conversation now. I didn't know what to make of it. Joseph had obviously told her about the bird memory. Had he told her about the "Green . . . head hurts"? If not, the emphasis on head trauma was striking, even with the recent inquiries of the hospital. Was the imagery in trance a memory of falling out of a tree at camp? Or was his mother's tale of the camp calling a way she had covered up something else at the time? If she really knew nothing about abuse, why wouldn't she ask Joseph directly about such a statement? Obviously, I would now. Despite my implied acquiescence with her request not to tell him she'd asked, I thought it was better to be open with my patient about why I wondered. It seemed especially necessary to explain the question because I remembered having asked a similar one at our first meeting. Then Joseph had told me no.

In the next session, I did tell Joseph about my talk with his mother. He'd already heard this from her. I summarized the conversation about head injury, which he'd also heard from her during his hospital stay. "She wanted to know if you'd talked about being abused as a child," I added.

This elicited a surprised look. I continued, "She told me you said you'd been abused to the family therapist at the hospital."

The look of puzzlement left Joseph's face. "Oh, yes," he said in a tone that implied "Oh, that little matter."

"You didn't tell me when I asked about traumas."

"No, this wasn't particularly traumatic."

"Would you tell me about your 'nontraumatic' abuse then?" This sounded a bit sarcastic the moment it was out of my mouth, but he smiled pleasantly.

"I was at the aquarium once with my grade school class. There was a moment when I was separated from the others in this dark room with all the fish tanks. A man came up behind me. He put his hand on my shoulder and rubbed himself up against my back. In retrospect, I'm pretty sure he was masturbating—a *frotteur*, I suppose," he added with his usual literary precision. "I didn't figure it out until I hit puberty; at the time I just thought it was strange. I wasn't upset really, just completely puzzled as to why he seemed so intense about this rubbing. But I guess that qualifies as sexual abuse."

"And is that the only abuse you ever remember?"

"Yes." I had to acknowledge his concept of "nontraumatic abuse" was fairly accurate.

"You didn't tell the therapist at the hospital the full story?"

"That's all they asked that first session. A few days later, when my parents weren't there and my speech had improved, they wanted to know the details, and I told them."

"And you didn't tell your parents what you meant?"

"They didn't ask." I was wondering how much to comment on the odd communications within the family when Joseph startled. He stared in horror at the corner of my office.

"What's the matter?" I asked.

"It's one of *them,*" he said with alarm.

"A White Person?"

"Yes."

"What is it doing?"

"He's just standing there, looking at me."

Curious about the nature of the hallucination, I stood up and raised my arm between Joseph and the corner. "What do you see when my arm is in front of him?"

"I can't see the part of him that's behind your arm," he said as if stating the obvious. However, organic hallucinations often superimpose themselves on anything in the visual field.

"What happens if I move to where he is?" I asked, starting to walk to the spot where Joseph's eyes were fixed.

"He's gone," Joseph announced before I got to the corner.

"Did my moving there make him disappear?"

"No, that's about how long they're usually there."

"Do you know of anything that makes them go away?"

"Not really. If I walk out of the room, I leave them behind, and they're gone if I wait awhile to go back. Usually I just stay there and they just vanish—*poof*—while I'm watching them."

I thought the little exercise had yielded some information. However, Joseph was uninterested enough in it that I wondered whether I'd actually needed to prove to myself that the White People could be walked through. His fixed stare had produced a compelling sense of someone being in that corner. After a bit more discussion while I waited to see if the figure would come back, I suggested we use hyp-

nosis to explore the bird memory. Joseph agreed. I did an
induction and suggested, "Go back to when you were
about six and riding to the beach in your parents' car. They
are in the car with you and your sister. You are all on your
way to the beach. Can you see the scene?"

"Yes, I'm sitting in the backseat with Penny. Dad's
driving, and Mother's in the front beside him. Penny and
I are playing a game, counting different kinds of cars."

"Very good. Now is there something about a bird?"

"We're counting cars; I've got three Corvettes already.
We are talking about how we're going to build sand cas-
tles." He continued to narrate detailed conversation for a
while before exclaiming, "A bird! A bird flies down. Oh,
no, it's going to hit!" He fell silent for a minute. "Did it hit?
I saw it hit, but I saw it miss. I can't ask. Dad stopped and
took my towel out of the trunk and wiped it off. But, no,
he didn't stop. Did it hit? Is my towel still there? It happened both ways. I can't ask, but I'll know when we get
there. I'll look in the trunk. If the towel is still folded and
clean, it didn't hit." He fell silent.

"Now let yourself see your family get to the beach—
can you see that?"

"Is the towel there or not?" he repeated, ignoring my
question.

"Can you see arriving at the beach?"

"No," he replied.

Although the hypnotic age regression was working to
some extent, Joseph was peculiarly inflexible in his experience of it. I took him back to the bird scene again and
tried to slow it down or take it further. However, each time
I got the same monologue in approximately real time. It
always stopped en route to the beach. Eventually, I sug-

gested that he let himself move to another scene that might tell him more about his experience of not knowing what happened to the bird. Immediately he moved to something I had heard before.

"Green," he said. "Head hurts."

"Where is the green?" I asked. This time more details were forthcoming.

"The floor . . . the kitchen floor. It's in front of my face and it's green," he said in a childlike voice. "Head hurts."

"Do you see anything else?" I paused as he moaned softly. "Is anyone else there?"

"Mom's yelling, 'What did I tell you?' I didn't pick up, so she's yelling . . . bleeding . . . blood."

"You're hurt?"

"Mom threw me."

"What happens next?"

" 'It's time for a nap,' she says. She takes me into my room, tucks me in. My head hurts." Joseph moaned and appeared in enough distress that it was uncomfortable to watch. "Mom's there with a rag. . . . Ouch."

"What is she doing now?" I asked.

"She's wiping blood with a rag . . . gentle, but it still hurts. 'Did you dream you got hurt?' she says. I dreamed she threw me." That was a chilling way to reframe the event—if indeed it had happened. "She's wiping the blood with a rag and tells me to take a nap."

"What happens next?"

"I'm a little owl."

"What?"

"My head hurts and I can't sleep. Then I'm a little white owl way up in a tree and I get sleepy." Joseph's voice faded in a manner suggestive of falling asleep.

"Okay, just rest as you leave that scene behind. When you wake up in a minute, you will be able to remember as much or as little as you wish of it, but for now leave it behind." I counted him awake.

"Do you remember what we were just doing?" I asked him.

"No."

"Nothing?"

"No." Joseph rubbed his head and grimaced.

"Does your head hurt?"

"No, it's fine," he said casually, although he continued the gesture for a moment longer, which I thought suggested discomfort.

"You were talking about green again." I recounted the sinister but surreal tale.

Joseph appeared mildly disturbed but not surprised. "Do you remember anything like that happening?" I asked him, "Either a dream or real event?"

"No, it sounds vaguely familiar as you say it, but I think from the hypnosis just now."

"You said you were a little owl up in a tree."

"Oh yes!" Now his eyes brightened with recognition. "That's how I used to fall asleep when I was a kid. I'd forgotten all about it."

"Can you explain the owl part?"

"I would have trouble falling asleep; I'd just feel tense. The thing that would always help me was to pretend I was a little owl way up in a tree. I'd feel like I really became an owl. Then I could relax and go to sleep. I did that for years when I was really young."

"I wonder how that relates to the bird at the beach?" I asked.

"Oh, yeah, although that was a crow or at least some kind of black bird."

"And was the white owl that you imagined becoming anything like the White People?"

"Only that they're both snowy white."

"Hypnosis can bring back real events you've forgotten—which seems to be the case with your sleep ritual. But people also imagine things or remember them in distorted form. Do you have any sense of whether the scene in the kitchen was a real event and you were being told you dreamed it? Or whether you remembered a dream about being injured in the kitchen? Or whether neither happened?"

"I'm not sure," he said softly. It was the end of the hour, and we were interrupted by the doorbell.

"That's my girlfriend," Joseph said. "I told her to drop by here 'cause we're going to a poetry reading together."

"Erica?" I thought they'd broken up.

"No, my new girlfriend, Tara. She's great. We're keeping it kind of low-key 'cause the last thing I need after Erica is a lot of intensity, but Tara is really nice to be with."

I'd buzzed the caller in as we spoke, so she now appeared at my office door. Tara was pretty in an impish sort of way, with tufts of purple and green hair sticking up amid her natural brown in a common college fashion of the day. Joseph introduced us, and Tara immediately remarked on the art in my office—two Leonora Carrington lithographs. The obscure surrealist turned out to be one of her favorite artists, so we chatted about this briefly before they left. She seemed bright and charming, as did all the women around Joseph at first take.

He arrived at the next session and immediately launched into an account of a conversation with his sister, Penny. "I called her up to ask about some of the things from hypnosis. She told me a lot. She's younger but remembers more about our childhood than I do. I asked her if she knew anything about my getting thrown on the kitchen floor. She didn't, but of course she would have been an infant then. But she did say, 'Mom had a really scary temper, don't you remember?' I didn't.

"Penny described a lot of times when our mother would fly off the handle. She said when Mom got enraged, it was like she was a completely different person. Then she'd act like nothing happened later. Penny was surprised that I didn't remember. She thought I just didn't like to talk about it, not that I'd forgotten. She told me a lot of bad stuff, although nothing where either of us got injured, like in that image last time."

"Do you believe your sister is remembering things right? Did her talking trigger any memories for you?"

"I'm sure what Penny says is true but, no, I didn't remember any of it directly."

"I thought we might do some more hypnosis today to try to get more details and especially to explore how it ties into seizures—and to the loss of reading and writing. The imagery came up in that context, but I'm not clear how it's related."

"I'm so tired this afternoon, I'm not sure the hypnosis will work." I looked at him questioningly, wondering if we were going so fast that the process was eliciting some resistance. Joseph explained, "The nightmares were terrible last night, so I barely got any sleep."

"Do you think they were worse because of last week's hypnosis or talking to your sister?"

"Not necessarily; sometimes they wax and wane without anything being stressful. I just saw Dr. Hartmann and he gave me a prescription for Tegretol. I'm ready to try it again. And I'm happy to do hypnosis. It's just that I may doze off now when I let myself relax."

"That's okay. Let's try anyway. If you're tired, maybe it would feel better to lie on the couch." I thought if he had a nightmare in my office, I'd at least understand it better and might be able to influence it.

Joseph lay down. I began the usual induction. Instead of a trancelike dissolution of muscle tone, I observed the fine twitches that accompany the earliest stages of sleep. When I notice someone beginning to doze during hypnosis, I raise my voice. That often rouses the person enough to enter hypnosis rather than sleep. However, today with Joseph, I did the opposite. I spoke with an even more soft, lulling tone. "You are going deep into a sleep-like state . . ."

He twitched more and then was still, breathing slowly and heavily. "Raise your right index finger if you can still hear me," I suggested. There was no response. I waited quietly to see what would happen.

Joseph gasped softly. I remembered that Erica had said he did this with the dreams. Then he gasped much more loudly. His body remained completely still, but his breathing was a struggle, like that of someone drowning. It didn't resemble any specific medical emergency that I recognized, but the effect was alarming.

I forgot my desire to observe a nightmare as my visceral alarm grew. I knew this was probably the way he always breathed during the dreams, but it didn't *sound* safe. Feeling an overwhelming urge to awaken him, I called out, "Are you all right, Joseph?"

An icy, electronic voice hissed, *"He's not here."*

I knew it had to have been Joseph who spoke. And of course I recognized the content from Erica's description. She was right that her imitation had not done it justice. The voice did not sound human.

"Joseph!" I said again as the situation took a moment to sink in.

"He's not here."

By this time I'd adjusted to the bizarre communication. "Where is he?"

"He . . . is . . . safe," the cold voice hissed with a slow, robotic cadence. *"He . . . will . . . return."*

"Who are you?"

"We . . . are . . . un . . . known to yours. We . . . have . . . no harm."

"Joseph is not able to read or write. He's a writer, so this bothers him a lot," I explained, sounding as inane to myself as the voice did spooky. "Can you help him get these abilities back?"

"We . . . try." We *will* try? We *have been* trying? It was hard to tell which; the White People didn't use tenses with all their verbs. I was ready to ask more when Joseph gasped and started as his eyes opened.

"I had one of the nightmares," he said, in a panicked voice. "I was in a waiting room with parents and babies. I would take a baby from its parents and reassure them it will be okay. I go into my office with the baby. It's an

enormous, gory room with dead babies impaled on
stakes. I ram this baby down on the next spike and go
back out to get another." He shuddered.

"You spoke."

"Did I?" he responded hesitantly—conspicuously not
asking, 'What did I say?' Still I persevered.

"You said, 'He's not here.' You talked in a really different voice," I reported, in a vast understatement. "I
asked about getting your reading and writing back. The
voice you were speaking with said something about trying. Do you remember that?"

"No!" Joseph did not now show any of the calm perspective that had been there for the equally disturbing issue of whether he had abuse memories. Neither of us was
inclined to try hypnosis or sleep again that session. We
used the remainder of the time to talk about long-term
plans. Joseph was scheduled to be in Boston for only one
more week before he left for the writers' retreat. Yet he
obviously couldn't write, so he was undecided whether to
go there to be in a more relaxing atmosphere or to stay in
Boston. He discussed the pros and cons for the rest of the
hour. Still uncertain when it came time to leave, he scheduled next week's session.

The following morning, I had an anxious message from
Joseph on my answering machine. "I've been seeing a
White Person. He's been here for two hours. Usually it's a
few minutes. This time, if I leave the room, he follows
me."

I phoned Joseph but there was no answer. I called
Ernest Hartmann. He'd gotten two distressed messages

from Joseph but hadn't been able to reach him either. Dr. Hartmann had left instructions for Joseph on the dorm room machine not to take any more Tegretol—just in case. He doubted whether it could cause this effect, though, and Joseph hadn't had any side effects from the drug before.

After my last client, I found another message from Joseph. "This is really creepy. He follows me all over campus and hangs around no matter how many other people are there. I *really* don't like this." I called, ready to offer a late session to see if hypnosis would make the apparition leave. However, Joseph was not in all evening.

The next morning, Dr. Hartmann called to say he'd spoken with Joseph, who had stayed the night at Tara's. He hadn't slept and was still being followed by the White Person. Dr. Hartmann was thinking about putting him in a psychiatric unit. I was alarmed at this idea but he said Joseph was willing to consider it. I asked if he thought Joseph was suicidal or dangerous. Hartmann said no, but that his anxiety was reaching a level too awful to tolerate outside a hospital. I did remember how panicked he'd looked when he saw a White Person for just a minute. However, hospitalization hadn't helped much the last time. As we were talking, Dr. Hartmann's call waiting clicked through, and he said it was Joseph.

I waited ten minutes and then called Joseph. My anxiously concerned tone met with an unexpectedly calm response. "I just told Dr. Hartmann, it's okay. I can read. The White Person is gone. He just vanished. In the same instant, all the books in the room had titles instead of gibberish on their spines. I opened several. I could read them all perfectly. I practiced writing something. Everything's fine."

"How do you feel?"

"Tired. It was awful, but I'm okay now. It's even in time to take the makeup before exam period ends so I'll graduate. I need to take a nap, and then I'll start studying. I guess I'll see you next week even though the problem is gone."

"Yes, I'm sure there will be plenty to talk about."

I talked to Hartmann later that day. He wondered if both the twenty-four-hour stalking and the return of the language could have been due to the Tegretol. I speculated on the possible effects of the hypnotic imagery. The conversation with the eerie voice "trying" to get Joseph's language back seemed even more relevant. If this were the cause of events, though, the delivery man had certainly hung around longer than I'd intended.

"How are you doing?" I asked Joseph the following week when he arrived.

"Really well," he said with enthusiasm. His voice now included a full range of natural inflections. "The exam was easy. I've started on the synopsis for my novel. Everything's going just fine."

"Is there any remaining problem with the reading and writing?"

"No."

"What about the nightmares and the daytime sightings of the White People?"

"They're much better, but I've had both in the past week. Even when they happen, they don't bother me as much now that I can work on the novel." There was no sign of performance anxiety about his writing—which of course had always been one of my hypotheses about why Joseph might have lost his language days after receiving the writers' retreat fellowship.

"Was that what you were sitting down to write when you had the seizure?" I asked him. None of the versions I'd seen of the history made this clear.

"No, I was writing a minor term paper—my last for the semester. I don't remember doing it, but I found the file on my computer half done with the date and time of the seizure. I finished it and handed it in."

"And Erica—you hadn't just spoken with her then?

"No, I've nothing to say to her. She's been claiming such obnoxious things about me to all our friends that I'll just be glad to be in another state from her."

This did not fit my brief impression of Erica from my phone conversation. But then almost nothing in Joseph's life was what it seemed at first. All through the treatment, I'd been weighing whether the pressure of the novel or the breakup or both within the same week had precipitated his writing loss. We weren't going to figure it all out in this last session, so I wanted to spend some time discussing follow-up.

"I know Dr. Hartmann has given you a referral to a psychiatrist near the writers' colony. But that person doesn't do hypnotherapy. I wondered if you wanted to pursue more work on that."

"Not right now," Joseph said. "I know hypnosis worked well with me. It may have the most chance of figuring out what the White People are all about. It looked like we were getting at memories—I guess we can't be sure. But something seemed, well . . . sneaky . . . about exploring things that way. Like tiptoeing into the house through the back door. I'm glad I did it 'cause it probably had a lot to do with my having my language back. But I don't really want to explore those things more right now. Since I can write again, I just want to focus on the novel."

I suspected "sneaky" was an especially sinister concept for Joseph that resonated with secrecy in his childhood. Many things went unsaid. "Sneaky" also summed up the discomfort evident in his poem "The Company." I certainly wanted to let him take what he'd gotten back—reading and writing—and enjoy them. I never push uncovering past memories. Some people get an enormous sense of closure by discovering the roots of disturbing symptoms. However, there is also much potential to stir up a lot of difficult issues. I think this was what Joseph was sensing and wanting to avoid now that his life had calmed down. We said good-bye on a positive note.

I've kept in touch with Joseph, and I know the basics of his life since our last meeting. He put off contacting the therapist Dr. Hartmann had recommended for almost the first half of his year at the writers' colony. When he eventually did enter treatment with her, he focused mostly on getting over his breakup with Erica. Later he discussed the new relationship with Tara, who had moved out there to join him. He did not talk much about the White People, whom he was still seeing in nightmares and waking hallucinations. His new therapist tried to address this by putting Joseph on a very low dose of an antipsychotic medication. In response, Joseph lost his language abilities for several hours, although they returned without intervention.

"That was the beginning of the end of my relationship with the mental health profession," he told me. Nevertheless, he thrived. By the end of his fellowship year, he had finished the novel. When I last talked to him, it was about to be published and he was working on his second. He was still living with Tara, and they had set a wedding date for a few months hence. I asked about the White People. Joseph said the nightmares had gradually disappeared. The White People continued to appear in waking hallucinations about once a day, but Joseph didn't find them bothersome. "I've come to think of them as more angels than devils," he told me recently. "Like guardian angels."

So what am I left to think of them as? I don't believe in their concrete reality, although I don't pretend to have inside information on angels or any other supernatural beings. I've known completely healthy individuals, whom the hypnosis literature calls "fantasizers," for whom the ability to hallucinate is a very positive phenomenon. (I'll discuss fantasizers more in the Conclusion.) In Joseph's case, I do think the White People are related to his dissociation and conversion symptoms. He probably had to learn to use his imagination to escape some unusual stresses.

What were those stresses? I think it is likely that the scene of being thrown to the kitchen floor is a real memory or some slight transformation of one. However, it is possible that it is a major transformation of one. There is some suggestion in what he recounted that the traumatic part of it could have been a dream. His sister's recollections suggest there was something to be afraid of, but not necessarily as extreme as the scene on the green kitchen floor. Often when my patients check out with their siblings traumatic memories recovered in hypnosis, they get explicit confirmations that someone else has remembered the event all along. I have not seen with my patients the situation portrayed in the scenarios released in the publicity of the False Memory Syndrome Foundation of uncomprehending siblings who can't imagine how anyone could think such a thing of their parents.

In working with Joseph, I stayed away from leading questions, ("Is your father there?" "Is someone hurting you?") which research has shown to be the base of most fabricated memories. However, there can always be some confabulation mixed into trance imagery—the identity of an abuser can be confused or the event itself can be altered in some way. Whether it was the scene in the kitchen or something else, Joseph seems to have learned some tendency to dissociate. Something that last week of school reactivated these issues. My best guess is that it was a combination of the fellowship award, the stormy breakup with Erica, impending graduation, and physical stressors such as end-of-the-semester sleep deprivation. His professional success and his newer, calmer relationship with Tara seem to allow him to call on the healthier aspects of himself and to use his imagination more consciously and productively.

I think similar phenomena produce many of the alien abduction reports I mentioned at the beginning of this chapter. Some of them are elicited by extremely leading questions in hypnosis about extraterrestrials or spaceships before the subject has mentioned anything similar. Others arise spontaneously in people who have either extremely gifted, healthy imaginations or childhood experiences that have led them to use imagery as a coping mechanism. One of the comments from UFO enthusiasts that most distresses me is that the purported witnesses must be either literally correct or "schizophrenic." Joseph is a good example of someone for whom hallucinations are a part of his ongoing experience but who is hardly schizophrenic.

Conclusion

I wrote in the introduction that the cases I selected for this book unfolded in my office like plays. In contrast, routine hypnotherapy tediously chips away at an issue that is compelling to the patient—and becomes so to me as I get involved in his or her life—but is not the stuff of great drama. My typical case is someone whose smoking is traceable to physical addiction and hundreds of minor stresses. Over four hypnotherapy sessions, his desire to smoke diminishes, then ceases as we combine imagery of healthy new habits with simple suggestions about not wanting to smoke.

Another typical patient comes to me complaining of

low self-esteem and chronic depression. Over a year, I use hypnotherapy to help her develop imagery in which she gains mastery over challenges, interspersed with sympathetic discussion of the childhood slights that caused her problems in the first place.

I have my typical failures, too, most commonly an anxious patient who comes for a couple of sessions and then decides that exploring traumas or learning safety imagery are more trouble than the medication he's been taking.

If you want to know whether hypnosis would be useful for yourself or someone close to you, there are a few general guidelines. As I've stressed throughout the book, anyone with hysterical conversion symptoms—psychogenic blindness, deafness, paralysis, or any other dramatic physical symptoms in the absence of a physical cause—is likely to respond well to hypnosis. Hypnosis is also the treatment of choice for dissociative disorders and amnesia following psychological stress for the same reason: these are trancelike disorders that indicate the affected person has excellent hypnotic ability.

Most people, of course, are likely to consider hypnotherapy for more routine issues. I've used hypnotherapy to help patients overcome problematic health or study habits, phobias, and sleep difficulties. Weight loss, insomnia, smoking, and pain control can often be treated in a group hypnosis format or through training in self-hypnosis. Group hypnosis and self-hypnosis are not sufficient for someone working on difficult emotional issues, but they can be very effective and efficient if you are otherwise happy and just trying to change one bad habit.

Hypnosis is a direct route to the mind-body connection. Imagery of healing can influence physical processes. Living through different interpersonal experiences in trance will broaden your perspective on what is possible. Hypnosis may also serve to unlock your imagination and creative problem-solving abilities. An important consideration when choosing between hypnosis and other types of therapy is the affinity you sense for one method versus another. The average rates of success and relapse are similar for many modes of treatment—but that doesn't mean each one would be equally likely to work for you as an individual. Think about whether the techniques in the chapters you've just read appeal to you. You're likely to work much harder in a mode that you find interesting. You are not likely to benefit from one that frightens you.

How hypnotizable you are does affect therapy outcome, but, surprisingly, it's not as important as other factors such as your motivation to change. However, many people are curious about whether they could be hypnotized aside from the implications for therapy, so let me say more about this. First of all, hypnotizability is a relatively fixed trait. If you are nervous or distracted in your first hypnosis experience, you may enter deeper trances in later sessions. Most people do learn to go into hypnosis more quickly once they have practiced it a few times. However, virtually no one with very low hypnotizability to begin with goes on to become extremely hypnotizable. The precursors of trance ability are present from childhood.

In the introduction, I mentioned that the characteristics of hypnotizability—such as the ability to daydream and to selectively ignore external stimuli—are all informal trancelike phenomena of everyday life. I have done research interviewing two types of highly hypnotizable people and studying the different causes for their trance abilities. The first of these types have been named "fantasizers" by Cheryl Wilson and Ted Barber of the Medfield Foundation. They believe all highly hypnotizable people are fantasizers; I did find them to be the most common subtype. Fantasizers experience vivid daydreams. In childhood, they describe at least one, most many, imaginary companions drawn from storybook characters, real-life playmates who moved away, pets and toys who talk to them. Parents of fantasizers encouraged their children's fantasy play. One woman in my study told me that whenever she asked her mother for expensive toys, her mother's response was: " 'You could take this [common household object] and with a little imagination it would look just like that [two-hundred-dollar whatever-Susie-just-got].' And you know," she said, "this worked for me—although Susie couldn't always see it."

As adults, fantasizers become deeply absorbed in stories, movies, and drama. They are often oblivious to real-world stimuli. They're the ones you need to shout at to pry their attention away from a good novel or the ones who blink in surprise at finding themselves in a prosaic theater seat at the end of a movie. They prolong their experience of these events by incorporating them into their fantasy lives, conversing with a book or film hero for weeks afterward.

Their adult fantasy continues to occupy a significant part of their waking hours. They daydream throughout the performance of routine tasks and during any unoccupied time. Some superimpose these fantasies on more demanding ongoing tasks: "I'm listening to my boss's directions carefully, but I'm seeing the *Saturday Night Live* character 'Mockman' next to him imitating all his gestures." Their physical sensations are often triggered by visual stimuli. Show such a person a photo of a desert and he'll immediately feel hot and reach for a drink of water. Hypnosis is a natural extension of these phenomena; most fantasizers find it more vivid, but not unlike much imagery they do on their own.

The second type of highly hypnotizable person I term "dissociaters," although they are not necessarily troubled like someone with a dissociative *disorder.* These are people who know they daydream only because they are often startled when called on unexpectedly by a teacher or boss. Their mind has been "somewhere else," but they're not sure if it's been off in the imaginary adventures of the fantasizers or drifting in a void. In other words, blanking out is their concept of daydreaming. Dissociaters may describe being so absorbed in books and films that they lose track of time, but their memory of what they've read or seen is vague shortly after, whereas fantasizers have excellent recall years later for things that have captured their imagination. Dissociaters may experience physical sensations from imagery, but these are usually negative ones such as nausea when viewing a film set on a tossing submarine. Some avoid television news because seeing someone else injured is so painful. Most of the dissociaters in my study had a history of trauma or abuse in childhood.

Hypnosis seems amazing to dissociaters and they are prone to view it as the hypnotist's talent rather than their own ability. Fantasizers are almost twice as common in the general population, but dissociaters have been overrepresented in this book because they overlap people with dissociative disorders, such as Dolores or Terese. Hypnotherapy can help dissociaters be more like fantasizers by teaching them to take control of their imagery abilities.

A last piece of advice to anyone seeking hypnotherapy: Go to someone who is trained in psychotherapy, *not* a lay hypnotist. Most states do not regulate the field and anyone can call him- or herself a "hypnotist," "hypnotherapist," or even "certified hypnotherapist." These terms do not reliably mean anything. Look for a licensed psychologist, psychiatrist, or social worker if you are seeking hypnotherapy. Locate someone trained in the appropriate medical specialty if you want to use hypnotic pain control for dentistry, childbirth, etc. It is equally important to work with a competent professional if you are interested in group hypnotherapy or learning self-hypnosis. The most crucial point in selecting a hypnotherapist is making sure he or she is broadly trained in psychological issues, although of course you want this person to have specific course work and experience in hypnosis. Use the same judgment you would in choosing any psychotherapist, by feeling out whether this is a person you can communicate well with and trust.

Many articles over the years by hypnotists have touted hypnotherapy as "increasingly recognized" or "growing in popularity." During that same time, nonhypnotists have sometimes referred to it as "old-fashioned" or "less utilized." Best I can tell, hypnotherapy has held a fairly steady place among therapy modalities throughout this century. It has evolved to about the extent other therapies have. For example, cognitions—the subject's perceptions—have become more emphasized in hypnotherapy as cognitive therapy in general has increased. Hypnosis is used more frequently for stress reduction as that becomes a focus of Western medicine. Just as at the turn of the century, hypnotherapists are a minority of practicing professionals, but they are not hard to locate.

Two organizations in the United States keep lists of qualified hypnotists:

The Society for Clinical and Experimental Hypnosis (SCEH)
P.O. Box 26225
Indianapolis, IN 46226
Phone: (317) 562-1915

The American Society for Clinical Hypnosis (ASCH)
2200 East Devon Avenue, Suite 291
Des Plaines, IL 60018-4534
Phone: (847) 297-3317

Outside the United States, similar lists for most countries can be obtained from:

The International Society of Hypnosis (ISH)
Department of Psychiatry
University of Melbourne
Austin Hospital
Heidelberg, Victoria 3084
Australia
Phone: 61-3-459-6499

Acknowledgments

First, I want to thank my friend Ellie Tonkin for her insightful suggestions, deft editing, and heroic patience while reading multiple versions of this manuscript. Other colleagues and friends who contributed invaluable critiques of chapters-in-progress include Kate Horsley, D. M. Thomas, Morton Schatzman, Bill Domhoff, Larry Rosenberg, Joe Dixon, and my parents, John and Barbara Barrett.

My agent, Stuart Krichevsky, was the ideal guide on my journey through the labyrinth of trade publishing Elizabeth Rapoport, my editor at Times Books/Random House, was a delight to work with.

I'm grateful to all the teachers who shared their knowledge of hypnosis with me, most notably the late Gail Gardner, who was my supervisor and seminar leader during my internship. I learned a great deal over the years from workshops at the Society of Clinical and Experimental Hypnosis, the American Society of Clinical Hypnosis, and the International Society for Hypnosis. Their addresses appear in the conclusion.

This book owes its greatest debt to my patients—both the ones whose stories appear here, and all the others who shared their lives and taught me how to help those who came after.

DEIRDRE BARRETT, Ph.D., teaches at Harvard Medical School and the Cambridge Hospital and has practiced hypnotherapy for the last twenty years. She edited *Trauma and Dreams* (Harvard University Press) and has authored numerous professional articles and chapters on hypnosis and other areas of psychology. Dr. Barrett is past president of the Association for the Study of Dreams. She has lectured on hypnosis and psychotherapy in such countries as Israel, Kuwait, England, and Holland. Dr. Barrett lives and practices in Cambridge, Massachusetts.